Our best selves

A guide to self-discovery and growth

By David Torne

Printed by IngramSpark, Inc., in the United States of America.

First printing, 2024.
Second edition, 2025.

Neutorn LLC
8 The Green
Dover, Delaware, 19901

www.neutorn.com

ISBN: 979-8-9906378-2-5

Cover illustrations

ID 27487954 © Regina555 | Dreamstime.com
Igor Sarozhkov / Alamy

Dedicated to my family, whose patience and comprehension have always infused me with a sense of peace, even in the most uncertain times.

Contents

Foreword

By Mar Navarro

J ust by reading the title of this book, one of the simplest and probably the most important questions that human beings have ever asked themselves since the beginning of their existence in this world may come to your mind: What does it really mean to be oneself?

The answer to this question might seem obvious; after all, we have supposedly been ourselves all our lives. We could almost venture to think that the fact of being ourselves is a phenomenon that occurs naturally and automatically, from the moment we begin to be aware of our existence and start to occupy a place as individuals in our society. But the reality is often not so simple; if we are totally honest with ourselves, we may realize that we are not really being ourselves all the time. In other words, we are not being all that in our heart of hearts we feel we could be.

Over the years, our upbringing, our social environment and the experiences we have lived have shaped our identity and personality. These elements have contributed greatly to the fact that we have developed certain beliefs and limitations regarding who we are and what we are capable of achieving, thus blurring the crystal of our true essence.

Fortunately, once we understand that until now, we have been operating only from the level of the limitations and mental beliefs that we carry programmed at a subconscious level, connecting with our most authentic and powerful version is much simpler than we can imagine. At that point, life becomes fluid, easy and full of opportunities that never cease to amaze us.

I would like to invite you to reflect for a few moments on how nature works; do flowers wonder what they need to do to fulfill their life cycle? Do birds take flight and halfway doubt their trajectory? The answer to these questions may seem obvious to you, but as human beings we sometimes tend to forget that we are also part of nature and that due to our mental filters we often complicate things more than we should, when it really wouldn't be necessary.

There is an intelligence that guides and synchronizes perfectly all the actions that take place in our world, a vital energy that allows our body to function in a harmonic and balanced way without having to worry about everything that is happening in it at every moment. This is the same energy that is in charge of keeping our body and that of all living beings that inhabit our planet alive; at the level of our brain, it allows our hemispheres to synchronize, thus operating at an optimal level and helping us to cultivate new habits that are aligned with our true essence.

When we finally open ourselves to this marvelous intelligence and connect to it, we recover the power we received from birth and are able to use it to our advantage to help achieve whatever we set our minds to.

Can you imagine what your life would be like if it flowed easily like the current of a river, freely and without needless limitations?

To be oneself is to be like nature, it is as natural and automatic as breathing. As we gradually remove those barriers that we have been creating for ourselves throughout our lives without even realizing it, based on fear and force of habit, we will feel lighter, and we will get closer to that version of ourselves that we are looking for. This requires performing an exercise in honesty, it implies observing yourself without making any judgments and unconditionally loving everything you see. It involves detecting and identifying what you want and moving towards it because you know that your soul is asking for it and that it is your true destiny.

We live in an era in which we have become too accustomed to observing the lives of others, thinking that ours does not have the same value; however, it is our true purpose to live our lives to the fullest. Thus, it is only from the total surrender to ourselves that we can live a life according to our best version, a life with meaning for us with which we feel fully satisfied.

This book aims to become a valuable guide that can help the reader to identify everything that is holding him down or no longer serves his individual evolution, through a journey towards understanding how our brain and mind work.

It is time for us to put aside conformism and begin to achieve our greatest desires, unleashing the full potential within us and sharing it with the rest of the world. It is worth working to make this possible, since our best version will not only improve our own life but will also allow us to share the gift that is our existence with others.

When we are aligned with our true essence, we feel inspired to develop our purpose in the world, that for which we have been carefully designed and that makes us feel good every time we do it. If each of us were to make this same determination, we could only hope for a longed for earthly paradisiac world for all the beings that inhabit it.

Introduction

Since I was a child, I was known to ask a lot of questions. I wanted to know deeply about the workings of the world. Wanting to grow in a so distracted world is not easy—we all get distracted very easily, and often lose track of our true purpose and our true essence. Being happy is about doing what we are meant to do, and enjoying it while doing it. We all have a role: and it is our missions to find it. The aim of this book is to help all who really want it with all our hearts.

When I woke up and decided to explore life I slowed down to explore who I was—and my parents always greeted my actions with all their love. The year I survived is the same year that 9/11 went rogue. I had recently recovered from a life-threatening drowning only to expect the commencement of university while it was shrouded by one of the worst mass-murder actions of the last decades in this world.

Let us rewind some years. I was born and lived in a place where at my fifth year of life the worst bomb of the Spanish terrorists history was placed at a big shopping market just thirty yards of my home. I still remember I did not want to go to school through that path for fear somebody placed another bomb—and amidst the worst facets of human beings I had to find a place of my own.

When I was five I remember all was good, I thought.

"Well, now that the bomb was placed here, they will not repeat the same spot."

I had failed in the previous deduction though. While terrorists were putting bombs through all Spain I remember thinking.

"Well, who cares, anyway they will not put a bomb in my city."

Since the region I lived followed similar political ideals than the terrorists, I assumed it was a safe zone. And from that moment the bomb hit on the front building, I never dared to think, "Who cares, if it is not on my home."

From that moment on I never dared to think that this is not a problem of my own, because one never knows when the bomb can hit home. And this is why I write this self-guide compendium of sorts, so that everybody can pick a little bit of everything and make it part of his own. I invite you to read it and pick something of it, and maybe it may hit just in the heart. The story is told in plural because I am part of this with all; because once I tell the story I try to read and read it till it also changes something from my own heart; because it is not the goal that I only improve with it, but certainly that we all improve from it–and the world.

During our lives we have been born in certain environments; we have been born with certain traits and certain genetic characteristics; we have been taught certain things–we have felt a lot of things. Life has placed us in a given situation, in a given moment, and some things cannot be changed. Here is where we are, and this is who we are. Yet, surprisingly we still feel that certain aspects of our lives still happen because of our choices. Certain aspects of who we are are in our hands to be changed: from little attitude behaviors; to little goals; to activate small incredible power abilities that we want to use; and to change the feeling that we should be acting more thoroughly than what we are doing right now, and veer towards a destiny that is crafted from our souls.

For a lot of us it can be very upsetting to have that feeling of alienation, but we can change it. There is a way, and it is in there–we just have to work for it.

So, what is this hardship that we are talking about? When we wake up we almost act automatically every day of our lives. We do have moments where we think we are choosing things; where we may sit very calmly deciding what we want to do. We would be surprised how our entire day passes and we just decided very few things. Most of the day feels like automatic–from the way we wake up, to the time we go to eat. Not many decisions are chosen consciously. Even sometimes, things that look like decisions are already automatic.

Let us say we want to choose what to eat today. We already know we have a diet that we decided a long time ago, so we will choose certain foods and not others. We already decided what kind of foods are tasty and which ones we do not fancy. It looks like we will decide what we will eat today, but it is mostly what was decided by us long ago by the diet we chose to have, the daily life issues, and routines.

Sometimes we have to make hard decisions. There are moments that we are forced to choose, but most of the time, though we could choose, we just do not. We just wake up, let our habits take the reins of our lives, and we just go along. We really choose to do the less tiring action–and this must stop. Why must it stop? Because sometimes, when we are calm and sit down looking through the window, we can see that our lives are not what we expected. We may do the same and the same and never change in a deeply felt way. We may see that we are already set up in this environment with little hope that we may be able to do anything about it –but little we know that there is also nothing stopping us from getting out from it.

We must also realize about reality. A reality that there is a physical world around us that has certain rules; rules that we can play with and force them to lead us, slowly but surely, to the place we want to be. The only secret is understanding those rules, and understanding what that place is that we want to be. The secret is changing all those aspects that we would love to change and we may think that they cannot be changed.

Some aspects are part of the environment that we must live in–but that does not have to stop us from living who we want to be. The only secret is wanting it and feeling that what we are living for is part of who we deeply are. If it comes from the heart, chances are it will be part of the path. If we want, with effort, we will be who we desire. The only prerequisite is being sure of what is what we really want, and the only condition to keep it is monitoring it close and never give up.

This book is addressed to all the persons who want to know what daily mindset to have so that, little by little, the world keeps changing around them in a positive way. This book is to become the person that we wanted to be and, if not that exact person, at least certainly reach that potential that has been hidden inside of us, but was never able to flourish at its best.

I hope that by reading it we all will be able to maximize all the qualities we know we already had, but we were never able to quite fully express. We will also be able to get rid of all those vicious automations that are affecting our life, yet for some reason we never paid attention to deracinate. Finally we will understand how the habits are formed, and how surely and maybe unconsciously we end up in places that at times we never wanted nor expected to be, but can be redirected to a place where we feel good and at home.

We will explore it more in a physiological manner, and at the end with psychology—which both are relatively recent sciences. But first we will go deeper, certainly in time. We will go to the knowledge that has been transmitted to us through the Torah / Bible by G-d to Moses at Mount Sinai. It is wisdom that, though ridiculed by some, it has certainly shaped all western society for centuries—and it has very cherished pearls on how to be the best we can be.

We will explain what the need for these techniques and this knowledge is, what the hardships that we may encounter are, and what the usual impediments that difficult our daily effort are to be the best we can be.

Finally we will show what the solutions to all this process are, and how we can achieve them in a remarkably simple and effective manner. We will learn some things that we can apply and will change us, slowly but surely, to be the person that, not only we wanted to be, but that it is also the best person that we can be—which is a lot.

To reach to those solutions–and to even apply the simple awareness technique–we will need to dwell a little bit on how the mind works; how the brain works; how it processes information; what are the different parts of the brain; how it registers rewards; how it decides what route to take; how to change that route; and all in all how we can act on that part of the brain process so that we end up doing the things that we really want–and we want to do them without much thinking, and almost in automated way.

We will work on a particular technique consisting of being aware–understanding and visualizing what are the consequences of every little thing we do. We will learn how we should prioritize our efforts to handle first things first. We should have in the back of our minds this understanding of how every action is shaping our brain and affecting future actions. With that simple conscious awareness at every single time–or in very important moments–we will be able to change ourselves unknowingly until we become the person that we were always yearning to become. We will do it not only until it becomes a reality, but also until it becomes part of who we deeply are.

We will be able to adapt to new situations that we did not expect. We will know how to constantly shape ourselves to the new surroundings; to the new requirements; and to the unexpected setbacks in a very fast and surely fashion. All this based on the deep awareness of what is really going on every time we do an action of our own will.

We will put examples of how this process is applied; we will make a little plan about what is what we want to change and who is the person we want to be; and we will understand how to identify and analyze what are our innate strengths–which mostly are already embedded in us and fixed, but can be identified, sharpened, and used. We will also analyze our failings and shortcomings–things we are not good at–and what we can do with them, or even if they need to be dealt with after all. And finally we will learn how to maintain and keep always developing these achievements while we also share the best of ourselves with the rest of the world.

I hope that we all enjoy this journey, and that this book becomes a right tool for anyone interested in self-discovery and growth for years to come.

Torah / Bible

How does growth relate to the wisdom of the Torah / Bible? This spiritual wisdom deals, among other things, with behavior. It has been around for more than three thousand years. It comes from G-d and taught to Moses on Mount Sinai. For those who know about the Torah / Bible this will be a reminder, and for those that are not as spiritually inclined it will be very useful to read. This is because it is wisdom that has been practiced for centuries, and has helped thousands and thousands of people with a clear success track. It agrees with the physical reality that exists in our brains, and it matches the reality of our surrounding world. We will use it to get the necessary steps to succeed. We will extract from it information on how successful people before us used this wisdom, and successfully achieved their goals.

1

Adam and Abraham, the power of beginnings

Adam is the first character we encounter. His first encounter with free will is met with a simple test: not to eat from a certain tree. His test is a test we encounter all the time where the best attitude is thinking calmly of the good and bad that will really come out of it.

Adam failings became our failings, because nowadays we are all Adam in a way. Our correction of his primeval sin is the correction now entrusted to us all.

Abraham is the source of the world acknowledgment of only one G-d. Even eastern religions, unbeknownst to most, originate in the sons that Abraham had with Keturah, also known as Hagar, the Egyptian princess [1]. He had six more sons besides Ishmael with her; and they left to the East endowed with presents. Those presents are mystical knowledge that were given by Abraham to his sons [1]. Now some may have shifted, but reincarnations, meditations, and even energies and elevations originate on deeper mystical knowledge that only the most advanced master.

They both are the beginning of most of our missions–as humans, and as nations.

Thus the heaven and the earth were finished, and all their array. By the seventh day G-d completed His work which He had done, and He abstained on the seventh day from all His work which He had done. G-d blessed the seventh day and sanctified it because on it He abstained from all His work which G-d created to make.
(Genesis 2:1-3)

We start our journey with creation itself, but as we can see what we assume as almost existing since ever, which only applies to G-d, also has its origins. The concept of weekend, for example—or a day off from work—dates back to ancient times. As soon as the civilizations adopted the scripture's wisdom, they started instituting one day of rest; each one different, from Friday to Sunday, but conceptually being a day of rest for all.

The day of rest has its origins in scripture. Before no culture practiced any day of rest, albeit for practical reasons like taking a bath, or selling goods on the market—this is what happened in ancient Rome [2], and only every nine days or so.

Interesting enough nowadays most of the world has two days off a week. The United States started having the entire weekend as days off from work because some people rested Sundays, and others Saturdays for their own religious observances [3]. Britain unofficially was doing it a decade before with the Industrial Revolution. Being the dominant countries after World War II, it did not elapse too long before the rest of the world ensued.

The concept of abstaining from work thus originates in scriptures. G-d Himself abstained from work after the six days of creation. The oral tradition transmitted to Moses by G-d, and passed down from generation to generation tells to take pleasurable meals and recommends studying and resting from all creative activity on this day. The day is also blessed. If one honors it by refraining from work, success awaits him during the week.

All this points out to conclude that in our plans and in our schedules we should include a day of rest; a day of abstaining from work where we let go of the mundane; a day where we stop and reflect about what we are doing; a day where we reconnect with our loved ones and friends; a day where we can enjoy some fruits of our labor, without stress, and in complete satisfaction.

This can be done on weekends or any other day, but being aware of why we work incessantly during the week is paramount to continue our path of growth. It is paramount that we reassess why we do what we do and where we are headed to. We need a time where we enjoy all that we worked for, and reconnect with other things that also matter.

The brain learns, and the habits adjust, but as we will see there is one element that makes it so, and that is the reward. Every week we need to enjoy that reward–be aware of that reward–with family, with ourselves, and with G-d. Like the brain, we need to let the connections form. We need to reconnect with our loved ones, with our wellbeing, and with our peace of mind. If we do not take these treasured moments to enjoy all our progress, or to assess what we do and to be happy, it will be very hard for us to be connected with our true purpose.

Another observation from this passage, as some physicists suggest, is that G-d's time is not our own time–at least when saying the creation lasted seven days. As some physicists realized, these seven days of creation are seven days when measured by a fixed time reference–or fixed pace of time–not the speed of time when the events were taking place.

In a study [4] performed by Dr. Gerald L. Schroeder of the MIT, he concluded that if we take into account the speed of time while the universe was expanding, it would show that seven days measured in a fixed time reference approximately six thousand years ago would equal all the billions of years that elapsed from the Big Bang to the seventh day of creation.

Based on his study, the seven days of creation that elapsed from the Big Bang until almost six thousand years ago, measured in a watch placed six thousand years ago, would have been measured as seven physical days indeed. Considering the speed of time was faster during the beginning of the universe formation, the watch placed on a fixed time reference six thousand years ago would have measured the almost fourteen billion years of creation as only seven days. When taking into account the effects of general relativity happening while the size of the universe from the Big Bang to six thousand years ago was smaller, the equivalence of a watch in a fixed time reference to one placed during its formation would be of seven days in one to almost fourteen billion in the other.

This is like having different watches. Our watch now where the universe has already expanded is moving at one speed. And another watch placed during the creation of the universe would move relatively much faster–with all around it. We say relatively because time moves faster or slower depending on factors like how big the universe is, or how fast we are moving. If the universe expands, time slows down. Shortly after the Big Bang time itself moved very fast, and the size of the universe was very shrunken, but as the universe started growing in size time itself started moving slower itself.

This is how physics currently understands it. Indeed GPS and other satellite technologies correct time for the speeds and gravity influence by knowing where the satellites are located, and at which speeds they go [5]. These corrections are what allows a precise map location in most smart phones nowadays. A watch in a satellite moves at different speed than on earth–and we refer to the speed of time. Both watches experience time at different speeds, like pressing the speed button of a playing video clip.

When it says the universe was created in seven days, it means exactly in seven days measured in a fixed time frame, like a watch placed six thousand years ago. The reason we do not feel the effects of time slowing down while the universe expands is because everything slows down with it. We just feel everything is the same because all the universe time pace slows down at the same rate. Only by watching the redshift effects on light coming from distant starts in an expanding universe we can deduce that the universe expands, and with it time slows down; much like we know an ambulance is distancing from us by the weird noise–lower pitch–the siren makes when leaving.

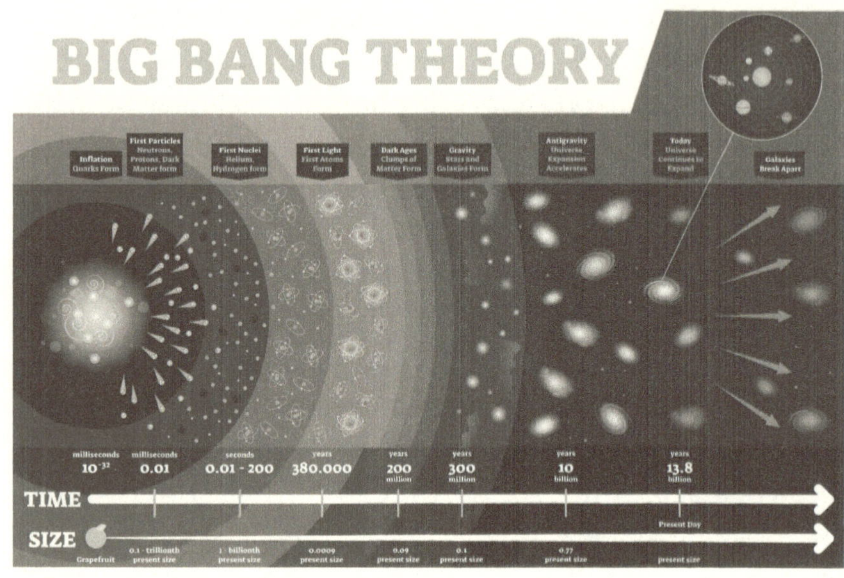

Time and space changes since the Big Bang
iStock.com/VectorMine

Billions of years of creation in a watch measuring it and existing since the Big Bang coincide with seven days measured in a fixed time frame located six thousand years ago. It is like watching a video at higher speed. While one watches the video at normal speed, the one playing it at two times faster speed has been able to watch the same video two times, or in half time from the other.

When we see a fossil of millions of years, it indeed experienced millions of years, but had it had a watch on it it would not have been fair to say it moved at the same speed than a current time watch. Relativity shows that the watch of the fossil was moving faster than the watch of our current time. So, millions of years would be measured in say a day in today's watch if we take into account how space-time curvature was in the past and how it is today.

The point is that the universe itself affects the speed of time, and when we say something lasted a certain period we must know if we are talking about a period measured in the time frame of the events happening, or being measured in a fixed time frame–like would be our current year with its state of the universe and its space-time curvature depth.

When watching a movie and the movie says the events lasted, say a year, we would see a difference between the pass of time inside the movie and the one measured by our own watch. Our watches would measure the real length of the movie in minutes, while in the movie the events would usually happen faster for the sake of focusing on key events of the plot. Events happening in a universe with a smaller size, like a movie, are faster than in our current universe state.

As we can see the seventh day G-d abstained from all His work that He created to make. It is recommended that we emulate Him and also make that day a day of sitting back and enjoying our job well done; a day of abstaining from all our work, and in particular all our creative work. Indeed there is a reason why we do work. It is good that we enjoy its fruits and its positive outcomes in its full capacity, for us, for our loved ones, and for all the world. May this rest bring us happiness, joy, and further success while we strive to be better in all that we do for years to come.

G-d said, "It is not good that man be alone; I will make him a helper corresponding to him."
(Genesis 2:18)

Since creation all animals usually have its pair. Adam and humans are no exception. Adam was initially created alone, since having time to live without a proper partner would help him understand the difference and need to have his other half.

Being with our other half is not only a way to not be alone or to have children. Having our other half just completes us–just makes us who we really are.

Since the dawn of creation we were created very special and very complete, but a lot of aspects of our life will just not fully mature unless we have found our other half–and we unite with our other soul.

Our missions will succeed up to a point. Our brain, our body, and our being will not be full until forming a union with our soulmate. The union of the souls requires not only that we join common missions, but that we choose somebody that is from the same branch than our soul–even though may complement us in a lot of ways.

The brain also has a special way of working for a woman than for a male. What one focuses on, the other looks at it from another perspective. While males tend to expand, women tend synthesize. It is not coincidence that when hiring high ranking positions, a married person is preferred to a bachelor. [6]

We may not control our destiny in full, and not having a partner is not always our fault: but we must be aware and take care of ours if we have a spouse. It is not for nothing that it is called "the other half": because once married, souls become literally one, even in heaven.

Therefore a man shall leave his father and his mother and cling to his wife and they shall become one flesh. (Genesis 2:24)

We are encouraged to marry as soon as possible. Leaving our father and our mother already hints that the next step is with our wife. The same could be said for a woman. The reason is because we will achieve more with a couple than alone. Generally in the world we could also assume that a couple living together is like married in a lot of aspects.

Marriage really acknowledges the union as a commitment to each other. Even while being a small ceremony, one is bonding to each other with witnesses of that commitment.

Spiritually it is said that with marriage the souls also bound into one, defining marriage as an official union with witnesses, where a token with value is exchanged, a contract, or a physical act–being all three practiced today as part of the marriage union.

Kings of ancient times like Abimelech would not dare to take the wife of another–at least that is what he expressed once he knew Sarah was Abraham's wife, and troubles entered his palace for it. Abraham knew that it was a common practice to kill the husband if a king fancied his wife–for such was the shame of a king if taking a married person. Knowing this Abraham said that Sarah was his sister when apprehended by the king's emissaries.

Abimelech gave a lot of wealth to Abraham in shame when he knew that she was his wife, but also as a public demonstration that he did not touch her–G-d prevented it.

Marriage bonds two souls into one in both planes–the physical and the spiritual. Indeed it could be argued that when Eve came from Adam both souls were one and the same, but were split as a female and male part. It would be one of our missions in this world then to unite again with our other half, at least with one that belongs to the same branch. More difficult yet is to keep that union by staying both in the same spiritual plane, growing with happiness and peace. It is the male who should procure her happiness. Indeed man has a lot of responsibilities–marital and economical wise. A wife should be treated like a queen.

> *G-d said to Abram, "Go for yourself from your land, from your relatives, and from your father's house to the land that I will show you. And I will make you a great nation; I will bless you, and make your name great, and you shall be a blessing. I will bless those who bless you, and him who curses you I will curse; and all the families of the earth shall bless themselves by you." (Genesis 12:1-3)*

Why is Abram told to change from one land to another? Could not he do what he needed to do where he was? Why does the place matter?

Places, people, and objects can be endued with holiness or lack of it. What does it mean? It means that what surrounds us exerts an influence, albeit subtle, in all that we do and think: from the place where we live, people we join, or even the decoration or objects we use themselves.

Abram was son of an idolater, but not only a common idolater—but the highest idolater priest. While he was young his father used to sell idols for the people. Abram knew using logic that there must be only one G-d, since otherwise the chain of creation would not make sense.

Abram grew in a very wicked area where idol worship and all sorts of practices were common. He indeed was thrown to a furnace after smashing his father's idols saying one raised above the other and smashed them to eat a client's offering. When his father said that that was not possible Abram made his point. It elapsed twenty something years before he was told to leave Aran by G-d.

Abram reached a point where his surroundings were hampering his growth in excess. He needed to leave the influence of his paternal family, place, and people.

One of the first things one must realize when growing is that the surroundings affect in a positive or negative manner. If a place, people, or else is not conducive to growth, possibly the effort will almost be unsurmountable. One needs to be surrounded with people that is conducive to growth. Excessive levity, jokes, or mockery certainly will hamper one from any serious endeavor. Wicked influences –or simply the lack of stimulating learning–tend to make it hard to change habits we really must get rid of.

It is not for nothing that a Nazir, one who vows to consecrate to G-d, stays for thirty or the committed days in separation from intoxicated substances–in particular wine. He must avoid all that reminds him of wine; avoid having his hair cut; and avoid being in contact with dead bodies until a final offering is given to finally become holy. He gains the status of holy since this period in separation elevates him enough to pass from his previous state to a loftier state: a holy state.

Abraham, after being told to leave, left with his wife to a new place–a place of growth. After growing and learning he became righteous enough to be himself the influencer. He used to give food to travelers and talk about G-d and about how to be righteous. He influenced all his surroundings, and was a source of blessings. All the people that blessed him, that is acknowledged his wisdom and appreciated him, were also blessed themselves. All who cursed him were themselves cursed. Maybe they looked at him with disdain–even animosity–or maybe they despised righteousness, but cursing righteous people is a recipe to get cursed.

Abraham was of the caliber to influence nations, and to merit even being father of righteous nations; such was his growth, such was his blessing. The first point is that we must be a blessing, and for that we must appreciate and identify sources of blessings–inspirational people. We must look for wisdom, goodness, and all the successful people whose knowledge and abilities can teach us–or even just move us.

Surrounding oneself with wicked people–or just mockery and levity–only brings curse and misfortune. Indeed Abraham himself in his kindness begged that if there were some good people in Sodom that they be spared death. There were not even ten righteous people, so there were not enough merits to save a whole city. Such is the power of righteous people. Only ten suffice to save a whole city as sinful as Sodom or Gomorrah.

Later we will see how many benefits righteous people get, but the blessings usually fall in all that surrounds righteousness. They bless things they do, people they join, and even while others do not have enough merits for it, by their merits others also succeed.

We must be a blessing and not a curse, and acknowledge righteous individuals or righteous people if we want to join those blessings too. We live as a society, and because things connect to each other, we want to connect to blessings, appreciate blessings, and get blessings.

Then G-d said to Abraham, "Why is it that Sarah laughed, saying: 'Shall I in truth bear a child, though I have aged?' – Is anything beyond G-d?! At the appointed time I will return to you at this time next year, and Sarah will have a son." (Genesis 18:13-14)

The first observance here is the issue of trust. Sometimes we put roadblocks in our path that do not exist. We have a destiny, and also paths to choose; and when we negate the paths that open to us we hamper our growth without a reason.

Here Sarah is justified in knowing she cannot have a child, but if G-d is giving hints that she will and are ignored, then it may become a self-created roadblock that hampers success.

Once we see we can do something that previously seemed not possible, disbelieving this is tantamount to make G-d angry, because it is our responsibility to follow the trails.

Our destiny is marked in a myriad of ways; from what we see, and from what we do not perceive. Abraham realized by the stars that he was not going to have children. There are destinies, but also ways to force some events. The lesson he was taught is that our actions and decisions can divert our destiny in big ways. Our small actions too may divert us and guide us to places that in our normal course of action we would never image would be possible.

We must never give up thinking we cannot change something. We have always free will. We are not aware exactly what we do control really and what we do not. We never know what actions really will trigger key events that will move reactions from above and from below. At the end we better treat it as if all our actions are our responsibility, and we have free will for all of them—even if in reality it is not always the case.

As an example of taken free will we have Judah, who was indued with a spirit that forced him to go and consort with Tamar. Tamar was his widowed daughter-in-law, who after losing her two husbands by levirate law was to be married with their closest single relative, Judah's only living son. Judah, after seeing his first two children die as her husbands, did not want to give her his third son for fear he would die too.

Tamar, being negated her rightfully owned husband and children, dressed as a harlot and enticed Judah by posing as prostitute on the road without him knowing who she was. She disguised herself from him to have a child from him. His free will was tampered and could not resist when enticed.

Judah accepted later the responsibility for her pregnancy when knowing the truth; before, she had been sent to be burnt. She sent word to Judah that the culprit had left her certain items in payment. Judah, the main judge at the time who was sentencing her to die by burning because he was told she was pregnant out of harlotry, realized by the items he was shown what had happened. He was the father of that child, and knew that by law he had been responsible to give her his son in marriage and he did not want to.

Tamar previous husbands refused to give her children by practicing onanism to not spoil her beautiful shape, so they were sentenced to death by heaven—so they died. Heaven directs events if needing so, but we must not disregard our responsibilities and our own free will: because we never know when it was our fault, or when it was just forced upon us.

Regarding laughter, Sarah was on a very high status. She did not know that the angels that told Abraham she was to have a child were angels indeed—since they appeared as common man. The point is that laughter is at times degrading, and degrades other persons too. This attitude is not liked in heaven—abusing laughter—because we insult other people. It is good to take pressure off here and there, but it is also a tool that can be used to degrade others, degrade the truth, and close oneself to valuable information. Indeed later it is shown that Abraham also laughed, but he did it out of surprise–happiness; to take pressure off from the situation. It is indeed necessary at times, but depending on how we use it, it works on the good side or on the bad side–intentions are everything.

Let us be truthful with ourselves and not put unnecessary roadblocks in our way. Let us be responsible for our actions, even if guided under different disguises– like masqueraded in an innocent laughter or more serious offenses. When we are truthful we laugh with good intentions and understand new avenues that open in front of us. We must accept that, though most things are handled in heaven, we are to be responsible for them all as if we had free will for each and every one of them. We never know when a decision is our real duty, or when it was just programed upon us. Even our most conscious efforts can be directed from heaven, but since we do not know which they are, we are to take responsibility for them all.

2

Jacob and Joseph, beacons of G-d in all lands

Jacob and Joseph are both entrusted with the task of living in the darkest places and sin entrenched locations while staying unscratched from their righteousness. Being righteous surrounded by evil required certain skills that other persons did not have–but they also had missions that other giants did not have. They had to bring light where there was none, bring wisdom where there was lacking, and also let others see that one just needs a little light to dispel much darkness. Such was the task entrusted to Jacob and Joseph.

> *Now you have known that it was with all my might that I served your father, yet your father mocked me and changed my wage a hundred times; but G-d did not permit him to harm me.*
> *(Genesis 31:6-7)*

Before Jacob went to visit his uncle Laban to find a wife, his brother Esau had an attempt on his life for getting his firstborn blessings from their father disguised as Esau. Esau sent his son to kill him for that. Esau's son did not want to kill his uncle, even if ordered by his father, but he could not say no, so Jacob told him that to save him he could rob him of all of his possessions instead–which he argued was equated to being dead. His nephew then, to spare Jacob's life, robbed him of all the big wealth that Jacob's father, Isaac, had given him to go to Laban and marry a wife.

At that moment Jacob decided to study fourteen years in the school of Shem and Eber before going to Laban. Studying for fourteen years taught him a lot. This is obvious by the fact that he understood with better acumen what was right and what was wrong. When working for Laban he understood that he was tricked and deceived by his uncle all the time, but he continued being honest nevertheless, and performed all his obligations. He cared even about the littlest details like taking responsibility for lost or damaged cattle with his wages, or taking care that his cattle did not eat from other's fields with utmost scrupulousness.

Laban had little livestock before Jacob came. Indeed, his daughter Rachel, future wife of Jacob, was watering the few cattle that her father Laban had when she first met Jacob. Jacob felt in love immediately with her, and agreed to work seven years for Laban to be allowed to marry her. While working to earn her marriage right he was tricked again and again by having his wages changed all the time. In the marriage canopy itself he was also tricked by Laban by giving him Leah, the older sister, instead of Rachel.

Jacob already suspected he might be tricked at the wedding, but Rachel, out of concern for her sister's humiliation, told the secret password she shared with Jacob to her sister Leah, and Jacob had no other way to distinguish her in the canopy. Jacob then unknowingly married Rachel's twin [7] sister Leah. Laban said in response that older sisters marry first in his country and gave him Rachel immediately afterwards as a wife on condition that he agreed to work for another seven years for him. Laban knew Jacob was honest and would comply with his part of the deal, so Jacob agreed to work for another seven years to pay again for Rachel's marriage, though this time he married Rachel first.

After fourteen years working for Laban he procured an enormous amount of cattle. Jacob was blessed with eleven sons, one daughter, two wives, two concubines, and an enormous amount of livestock that he grew over the years. His honesty and diligent work brought riches to Laban beyond Laban's wildest dreams.

Jacob stood trickery after trickery and kept being honest and working rightfully all the time. As the quote says, he was always protected by G-d. When Laban said speckled cattle were to be Jacob's share, all cattle were born speckled. When he was promised straight cattle instead, all were born straight. Jacob understood after his long years of work how to make cattle born straight or speckled, and at the same time he was protected from heaven from Laban's tricks and assisted in all his dealings.

The lesson here is clear: honesty pays off. After fourteen years of work he took the cattle which rightfully belonged to him. In a last dealing with Laban, where he was about to be tricked, Jacob outsmarted Laban and took most of the cattle respecting all the conditions imposed by Laban in the deal. Not only had Laban failed, but Jacob ended up rightfully with all the unpaid wages that Laban had withheld from him during all his years of hard work.

Jacob decided then that it was time to leave, so he decided to leave secretly with his cattle and family avoiding any more of Laban's tricks. When Laban discovered it, he decided to pursue him and kill him. Laban, himself evil and a serious idolater and magician, was in the road to kill him when he was suddenly warned by G-d in a vivid dream that he should abstain from killing Jacob. Laban did not kill Jacob and, moreover, by decree of heaven while leaving his home unprotected the first night, Laban was robbed of all the cattle he still had in his possession.

Jacob was honest and had blessings for it, blessings that profited him and all around him. Being honest is a paramount trait to succeed in business, but also to succeed as a person. We spend countless hours at work trying to earn wealth and doing our most skillful jobs. Honesty is one of the biggest duties we have during work and during our objectives. The end does not justify the means.

Being honest is being truthful; not taking money that does not belong to us; not deceiving; working our paid time in full; being careful when managing others' possessions; and controlling that our assets do not damage others' possessions either. Being honest is taking responsibility of our wrong doings. Indeed, it is taught that the first question we are asked in heaven is, "Were you honest in your business dealings?"

Honesty is part of our work, and this trait is one that we must learn, train, and practice till it becomes a habit to us. At the end, it is not so much the result, but how we reached our destiny that molds who we are and what really matters. Indeed, maybe the money we are going to earn is already reserved for us. The only question is, Do we want to earn it honestly or with fault?

They saw him from afar; and when he had not yet approached them they conspired against him to kill him. And they said to one another, "Look! That dreamer is coming! So now, come and let us kill him, and throw him into one of the pits; and we will say, 'A wild beast devoured him.' Then we shall see what will become of his dreams." (Genesis 37:18-20)

Joseph was going to be killed by his ten older brothers. Such is the animosity that can arise between brothers. One would think that he is younger and they should take care of him and not wanting to kill him.

Animosity builds up over time. Joseph was always the preferred from his father, and moreover he was a child from Rachel, the openly shown most beloved wife of Jacob. The reason to wanting to kill him is more profound. He openly said that, in a dream that he had interpreted, he saw that all would bow down to him, even his father—and that was a serious thing to say and believe as true. In fact Judah was to be the leader prophetically instead of Reuben, the firstborn brother who lost his birth right after sinning. Why was Joseph so bold saying that when his brothers had already been harboring feelings of animosity towards him for years?

Everybody had a vision of the other slightly distorted. Joseph would complain of mischief from his brothers, whereas albeit seemingly out of the law all they did was always legal and correct. Indeed, until the last moment the brothers were convinced that killing him was a correct thing to do because of all their deductions of what they thought their brother might do in the future.

Obviously the brothers were at fault, and Reuben and later Judah tried to save his brother. Reuben by throwing him into an empty pit and wanting to rescue him later himself, and Judah by proposing to sell him as a slave while a caravan of Midianites was passing to Egypt instead of leaving him to die.

This is one of the most puzzling events where the most righteous individuals concoct such a perverse plot. When they were older and observed the grief of their father, meditating about all they did, they all decided to look down on Judah, because he was the leader, older than them, and should have imposed himself more thoroughly on what was the right thing to do. Such is a leader's mission: to move people towards an end, with wisdom and care. Indeed, they craved for his leadership, and he let them down.

About the brothers though, envy, slander, hate, and anger really blind any person in any situation. It can put us in a story concocted only in our brains that is far detached from reality, and when we wake up to the realization of our folly, the shame is unspeakable.

The reality is that sometimes G-d puts us into situations and people to test us, and though people have free will and chose to do certain things, they only happen because G-d chooses to—be it as a chastisement, a lesson, or a test.

Here in the story everybody had an opinion of the opposing part, but none was correct–because judging positive is one of the lessons in scriptures. Assuming good till proven the opposite, and if in doubt investigating and discovering the truth is the way to behave, not the other way around.

The brothers could have assumed that Joseph was just telling them what he saw purely, without any hidden intention of overpowering his brothers in the future. And Joseph could also have assumed that his brothers were more righteous than what he was giving them credit for.

Later we will see that indeed all the brothers bowed down to Joseph; and Joseph grew and matured to the point of forgiving his brothers, because he understood that all is part of G-d's plan, and that all that happened was for the ultimate good.

The lessons are various. First, we should judge positively always under the doubt; assume the other part has good intentions; or that it happened in a good way that we may not foresee. G-d is the one who decides what everybody is able to do anyway, so if somebody does something, he must have the approval from heaven. That is why fearing heaven above all else makes sense–because all is in G-d's control, even when we are harmed. If we judge positively, we also assume G-d wants positive things to happen to us.

Another lesson is that things happen for good. In the story the result of all this is that all Egypt, Joseph's family, and the surrounding lands were saved from starving by Joseph, who became the de facto Pharaoh since he was given full control of Egypt. He became Viceroy, and had control of all the food of the entire land at the time.

Joseph had been sold as a slave, and in his leadership and beauty he served Potiphar, the chamberlain of Pharaoh's butchers, whose wife enticed him to sin till almost caving in. Potiphar's wife was like a model of the time, and Joseph was only around seventeen years old when he was sold as a slave. He refused her advancements all the time, and yet he was sent to prison accused of assaulting Potiphar's wife.

G-d's will decreed that he would stay a total of twelve years in prison. Joseph had raised in responsibility in Potiphar's house, and he had become a trusted leader—such that all of Potiphar's household was managed by him. The prison was a way to acknowledge that had Potiphar believed Joseph really forced himself to his wife, he would have been killed instead.

Joseph became gossip, and Egypt knew about him, Potiphar, and all his story. Even the story of Potiphar has a positive judgement too. Potiphar's wife saw through prophecy that she was predestined to have offspring with Joseph, but she did not see that her adopted daughter, Asenath, was the one predestined to be with Joseph.

Asenath happened to be the daughter of Dina, and Dina in turn was the daughter of Jacob and half-sister of Joseph. Dina had been raped in Shechem by the local prince. The daughter born of that rape was given as a slave to Potiphar while Joseph was in prison. Joseph would later marry her after seeing her wearing a Hebrew golden plate, and she would become the mother of two children who would later represent two of the twelve tribes: Ephraim and Manasseh.

At the end of twelve years in prison Joseph predicted a dream to Pharaoh, and he was so to the point and proposed a so thoughtful action plan afterwards that he was immediately proclaimed Viceroy of all Egypt. After interpreting the meaning of Pharaoh's dreams he devised a plan to use the excesses of the foreseen years of bounty to stave off a coming famine making Egypt very wealthy. His brothers then came for food to Egypt, and unbeknownst to them they bowed down to Joseph when entering and coming a second time after being accused of being spies. Joseph saw then that the dream he had as young came true.

We must always look on the bright side if we want to keep moving. Or we are tested; or we are redeemed for something we did; or something must happen so that in a chain of events an ultimate good ensues. G-d is in control, and all happens for a reason. The power to veer the situation is always on us, on our repentance, and on our good deeds. All we encounter in life is meant so that we gain our maximum profit, our maximum wisdom, and our maximum growth. A positive mindset and good expectations are always needed to cope with the nuances of life that we may not be privy to understand at first. Like Joseph, only in hindsight we can see that most of what we experience in life is for our ultimate good, and has a profound reason in the tapestry of life.

He cried in a loud voice. Egypt heard, and Pharaoh's household heard. And Joseph said to his brothers, "I am Joseph. Is my father still alive?" But his brothers could not answer him because they were left disconcerted before him.
(Genesis 45:2-3)

This part is one of the tensest of the entire book. The brothers sold him as a slave, and after twenty two years a severe famine in all the land forces the brothers to go to Egypt to buy food. Joseph was Viceroy of Egypt, and had saved food during seven years of plenty because he interpreted Pharaoh's dream foretelling the coming of seven years of famine after seven years of plenty. His brothers did not have that information, and were living the famine with the rest of the world.

The brothers came to Egypt to buy food, and Joseph, the Viceroy, accused them of being spies. So, they bowed down to him without recognizing he was Joseph, their brother. They all answered all the questions the Viceroy asked.

At the end, after tense encounters with the Viceroy and coming a second time for more food, he revealed that he was the brother they tried to kill and later sold as slave. The first question of Joseph was about the wellbeing of his father. Joseph did not know that Jacob was mourning him, nor that his brothers told his father he had died.

The brothers understood that all they had done, not only was wrong, but that Joseph was right–all bowed down to him as Viceroy of all Egypt none other.

Joseph understood that the dreams would be fulfilled; but the brothers could not see the master plot. They could not realize Joseph was a gifted interpreter of dreams and could foresee events by interpreting dreams when they were distinctively prophetical. Joseph did not see his brothers with revenge or animosity, he just knew from the beginning they were part of a story–a story crafted by G-d. And in one way or another, it would be fulfilled.

Sometimes we fail to see the masterplan. All the events are connected and lead to an end. Unrelated events later form a story that drives to a specific end, with a specific purpose–and we may be part of that story.

This and other stories have characters. The roles are given. And ones serve to chastise while others to dispense good. We have free will, and this free will is in a way the character we choose to be in the story. Story has evil tormentors when good people misbehave, and has heroes that stand the vicissitudes of life. We can all choose the role, but later the wicked are judge themselves–even while they served at the same time for a given purpose. We are judged for our good and bad actions while at the same time these actions we choose to do fit into a plot. And in a series of events they end up exactly where G-d wants them to be.

Nobody wants to suffer prison like Joseph, or being sold as a slave, but he understood his role, and he understood the end. He just did his part and never hesitated nor complained–even while in prison.

After ten years in prison Joseph predicted the dream of a butler, and he predicted that the butler would be exonerated for having served Pharaoh a cup of wine with a fly inside. Before being freed Joseph asked the butler to remember him, since he correctly interpreted his dream and intuited the butler was the conduit G-d was using to liberate him. The butler forgot about him though, and Joseph stayed two more years in prison. Later Pharaoh had a dream that nobody knew how to interpret and the butler recalled that Joseph interpreted his one successfully. And upon interpreting Pharaoh's dream correctly Joseph was liberated and made Viceroy.

When we know we are part of a story, we know somehow that it will go one way or another; and G-d will bring salvation if we trust Him and humbly correct our ways. Joseph knew that too, but after interpreting the butler's dream he begged the butler to remember him. We learn from oral tradition that G-d made the butler forget, and chastised Joseph with two extra years in prison for not relying on Him for salvation, but in the butler instead. When liberated though Joseph clearly told Pharaoh that G-d gave him the ability to know dreams, not himself.

The subtlety is that Joseph knew G-d would liberate him, but when he intuited the avenue Joseph chose to rely on that avenue and not in G-d. G-d could have prepared another way out, so he just got lost in the details.

In a lot of our endeavors sometimes we become obsessed with opened avenues, and lose sight of the bigger picture. We work hard in something, and after a lot of time and resources invested we see a clear consequence and an open avenue of success. When this avenue appears sometimes we look at it as if it were the one and only consequence, much like Joseph was very concerned with the butler and relied too much in him. When something fails, if it fails, we may end up in desperation, thinking we failed and we lost the opportunity. We may be missing the big picture. The butler is not the one who takes us out of prison–it is G-d.

Let us choose who we want to be, let us predict what is the role we are headed to, and let us let our work and trust be our guiding force. Let us let the events unfold, and the story be in the hands of heaven. That our goals, desires, and missions reach its best destination. And that we do all our part to make it so.

3

David and Solomon, wisdom from kings

David and Solomon had both tremendous wisdom. Solomon was gifted with the capacity to understand, distill, and apply wisdom to the world which had never been seen before. He could take the most complex concepts and give them to an unlearned person, or apply logic and wisdom to solve common life problems in creative manners. He was regarded as the wisest man ever existed, and certainly his wisdom is still used to this day.

Young lions may want and hunger, but those who seek G-d will not lack any good.
(Psalms 34:11)

Who are these young lions? A lion represents all the power and strength of the animal kingdom. He has skills to kill and yet, even as young and strong, he may want and hunger.

The young lion is the epitome of a person who has power and relies on himself; believing he does not need anything nor anybody else while lacking the acknowledgment of, not only who gave him these power and resources, but also who sustains creation.

Those seeking G-d are those who acknowledge Who is the source of everything. By the mere asking, even though naturally may seem less suited to receive it, they may get it, because the source is not in the strength of the requester, but it is from G-d, the limitless of the giver.

By understanding that even though we have resources the ultimate giver of good is beyond ourselves, we can surpass our limitations and we can also expect that setbacks that can come even to the most gifted person will be highly reduced.

Seeking G-d is seeking for His help, for His guidance. Once we acknowledge the source, seeking G-d is also understanding what He wants from us. It is understanding what actions that we do bring blessings from Him. Seeking Him means knowing all we can about Him and relying on Him as the source of all we have. The masculine manifestation of G-d is the providing attributes side.

Let us focus on the right values, the right attitudes, the acknowledgment of where all blessings come from, and automatically we will not lack any good. By good meaning what is really good for us.

The beginning of wisdom is fear of G-d, and the beginning of understanding is knowledge of the sacred. (Proverbs 9:10)

What does it mean to fear G-d? Why would this fear be the beginning of wisdom? Do we need knowledge of the sacred to understand things?

There is a feeling in most of us that there is a higher power or spiritual system that eventually rewards the righteous and ultimately punishes the wicked. If we identify the maximum source as G-d, then the fear or reverence for Him pushes us to understand what it means to choose right. If we do not have this fear or reverence for the consequences of not being righteous; or if we do not realize and understand that righteous people eventually succeed and wicked do not, we never walk on the right path. Maybe we do when we have reached unnecessary bottom pits, but then, of course, we must do a harder work to get out–at least without a modicum of pain.

A judge in ancient Israel could not be in a position of deciding matters if he did not fear G-d. Since they were the maximum authorities, the acceptance of a higher authority that always watches them prompted them to be weary of all sorts of bribes. They watched even the most minuscule miss-judgment. Even an insignificant good intentioned chatter that could favor one side without reason would be reason enough to voluntary disqualify themselves on a particular case. [8]

The reality is that we usually look for pleasures, be it physical, spiritual or of the loftiest and unselfish type, but we aim at a goal. The realization that good behaviors or righteousness and bad behaviors end up in different outcomes, even if physically we cannot say for sure why it turns out to be that way, is the first step to want to know more about the workings of the world–to understand it.

Knowledge of the sacred includes not only the entire scriptures, but also a lot of wisdom transmitted orally from generation to generation and that stays true to this day. Sometimes though some wisdom needs certain interpretation from learned masters to discern its meaning.

Go to the ant, you sluggard; see its ways and grow wise. Though there is neither officer nor guard nor ruler over her, she prepares her food in the summer and stores up her food in the harvest time. How long will you recline, O sluggard? When will you arise from your sleep? A little sleep, a little slumber, a little folding of the hands to recline, and your poverty will come like a traveler, and your lacking like an armed man. (Proverbs 6:6-11)

Here we can see one of the most straightforward teachings we can read. Laziness or sluggishness can take us directly to poverty or deep constant inaction.

If we analyze this proverb, the ant is clearly a laborious insect. The question is, Is laziness an inherited trait? We are not sure yet, but it is noted that certain persons tend to acquire the lazy habits faster than others. Laziness is one of those habits that, under the lack of will or clarity of what we want in life, fills the void slowly but surely till it seriously becomes one of the biggest bad habits to deter.

The consequences of this negative habit of laziness are clearly shown in this proverb, but the question is, How do we get rid of it? One of the best ways is to run to do any positive activity or thing before thoughts of laziness or comfort prevents us from doing it. Creating a list of markedly the worst moments where laziness stops us from doing what we should is a good way to be aware of the moments we must act instead of waiting, and to be ready to act immediately the next time the occasion comes around.

We should train our brain and body to act when the moment to do the activity arrives. In the beginning our lack of habit may make it harder, but that is why just doing the positive action immediately and without delay when its time comes avoids the excuses or the mechanisms laziness uses to stop us from acting [9]. Once we have accustomed ourselves to do the positive actions we already set out to do with calmness before, the resistance or laziness will disappear, because our bodies, minds, and hearts will already be used to it [10].

Let us get rid of these lazy thoughts by acting without delay, doing what we already thoughtfully set out to do. And in the case of hard tasks just break them into smaller chunks at first so that our bodies are better suited to handle them in the beginning. If they can be done smaller first, we will do them better next time, and at least we get used to them. The sooner we do the needed activity when the time comes, that is, between the moment we know we must do the activity until we do it, the sooner we will prevent laziness from hampering us ever more.

The deed of a righteous person brings life, but the produce of a wicked one brings lacking. To heed discipline is a path to life, but one who abandons reproof goes astray.
(Proverbs 10:16-17)

In this proverb we start distinguishing between the righteous person and the wicked, and how they affect whatever endeavor they do. Indirectly it also tells us what attitudes may bring us to become righteous, and which ones to be wicked, which seems to equate by extension to going astray.

Usually, having discipline and a constant mindset of growth lead one to be wise and to become righteous. The mere lack of will to improve, represented here in a person that abandons growing or opportunities of growth, is a person that will return to the wicked behaviors or, as they mention, to going astray. We will see later why growing or being righteous is a path of life. We could summarize that one of the main reasons why growing to be righteous is a path of life is that we bring life to ourselves and to all those around us, besides also fulfilling a correction, so to speak, of the world.

It is believed in even deeper spiritual levels that a righteous person brings this lofty state to all the endeavors he entertains. Objects that a righteous person creates get embedded with that spiritual energy, and are used for good –or somehow end up bringing life. Deeds and produce of the wicked get embedded with the opposite energy, and their destiny is naturally endowed with an unsuccessful use or a final lacking to do its intended purpose. That is why the produce of a wicked may end up bringing lacking, because fundamentally it is attracting a negative destiny.

Discipline is the way we correct our faults. Humbleness and acceptance of our mistakes is the first part to be open to correction, to success, and to life. Haughtiness usually is like a full vessel, we cannot fill anything inside because it is full, albeit maybe of useless content. Thinking that we are perfect and lack nothing is an act of folly, because to start with we avoid improvement, and certainly our own misunderstanding leads us to a derailed destination.

When others discipline us, while stemmed from a hidden source of love, we can profit from points of view that we were lacking, shortcomings that we were not paying attention, and best of all counsel that though hard to swallow is truly valuable. If we accept reproof in a good manner we can expect more guidance, otherwise we do not profit these moments of growth.

Let us choose righteousness and growth by accepting guidance and reproof when we are offered such. That our actions, creations, and activities infuse life to all of us and to all around us, and that we always return from a derailed destination from wherever is that we come from.

*It is the blessing of G-d that enriches, and one
need not add toil with it. It is like sport to a fool
to carry out his evil design; wisdom is like sport
to a man of understanding. What a wicked one
fears will come upon him, and G-d will fulfill the
desire of the righteous. When the storm passes a
wicked one is no more, but a righteous one is
the foundation of the world.*
(Proverbs 10:22-25)

The first sentence already tells us that G-d's blessings are
the ones that enriches, but it does not mean we should not
toil, yet we do not need to add toil to the necessary amount
to earn more riches.

This idea is hard to swallow, but we could also
understand that at times we are not aware that some of our
work is not really useful anymore. A tired day, where we
are being unproductive already and we keep pushing
ourselves for no reason, is an example of moments where
we should realize that it is time to stop already.

Spiritually it literally means that, if we want, we can do
extra toil, but the riches will be the same ones destined for
us. Is not easy to know where the limit is and when to stop
adding more labor, but I leave it as an exercise to the reader
to know where the limits is.

The fool uses his extra time to carry out evil designs,
understandably to expect more riches or benefits. The man
that understands that G-d does not expect from us extra toil

to earn more riches from the considered right amount uses his extra available time to acquire wisdom.

We see that the destinies of both are quite different. While the wicked may enjoy success temporarily, given a certain point, all vanishes like in a storm. The one who acquired wisdom seems to be equated to a righteous one. The righteous then is the foundation of the world, because that is why the world was created, so that we endeavor to be more than what we started with: to grow, to be G-d like.

A man of kindness brings good upon himself, but a cruel person troubles his flesh. The wicked one does false deeds, but one who sows righteousness has a true reward. One who gives sincere charity is consigned to life; but the pursuer of evil is consigned to his death.
(Proverbs 11:17–19)

Here we see that kindness brings goodness, and a cruel person troubles his flesh: we see the concept of a deed for a deed. One who creates goodness gets goodness in return; the one who causes pain receives a similar destiny. The wicked do false deeds, so their reward is also false—not a true reward; the one who acts righteously, gets a true reward—a real reward.

The concept of sincere charity already shows us that what one may appear to outsiders may not be what one really intends. G-d knows our innermost thoughts, intentions, and actions, so a true judgment is always done.

We also know what the reality of our actions is. Internally we know if we are acting with good intentions or not.

When saying sincere charity is consigned to life we know from other passages [11] that indeed it can also save us from a predestined premature physical death or illness. It is a life where maladies are side stepped, and it is more endowed with health: a path of life. Likewise, we could say that the pursuer of evil gets the opposite end: a path of death. Life is also meant as the eternal after life; and death would also be a physical death without afterlife.

We are working on personal growth, and it turns out this work happens too in a society—and some things come unexpected. If we accustom us to do sincere good deeds, we can expect the unexpected happenings to also be positive. This is a spiritual lesson that will smooth our path of growth and will lessen the deviations from our goals.

We can also read it in a way as the anxiety of what can happen. If we know we acted good, we are not worried about consequences that could occur later to us. If people sort it out, they will understand that we were acting with good intentions, and we are tranquil all along. If we have something that needs correction, we ask forgiveness, we correct it, and we go with goodness in our heart.

When there is worrying in a man's heart, he should suppress it, let a good thing convert it to gladness. (Proverbs 12:25)

It is hard to deny feelings that we may have—the reality is that worry is part of life. Sarah worried that she was old and that she still had not a child; Jacob worried that Esau might kill him when returning from his uncle's home; and the sons of Jacob, most involved in the selling of Joseph, once Joseph disclosed he was the Viceroy of Egypt, worried very much that he might harm them for having sold him as a slave in his youth.

Things happen, but often we create the extra worries— unnecessary worries. All is in the hands of G-d, and believe it or not He has our best interest in mind. If we have truly thought about our own misdeeds, stopped doing them, repented, and have since committed to do the right thing, we can only realize that all that will happen is the best thing for us.

If we do not correct ourselves, the pain may also be the best for us. All is a matter of knowing why anything that happens is always good for us. At the end we have free will, and we ought to choose right to maximize the good. If there is any action to take, we should take it, then focus on a good thing, and let this good thing convert any worry into gladness.

We have duties, and we have lots of positive things to be joyful for. We can choose to be happy or not at every single moment. Once we have dealt with a situation it is useless to spend any extra worries any more. Confidence that things will turn out good is essential for our life, overall if we know we are doing everything to be this way.

Since G-d is in control of everything, even of what people can do, if we do not put ourselves in needles harmful situations, then all the outcomes are exactly the best outcomes that will happen for us. This is simply because we have been put in the best way we and our soul will succeed.

Not denying that there is judgment or punishment, only that they are the most merciful and beneficent for us.

We must realize that G-d is in control of everything, and if we use our free will wisely, He will help us mend our ways and come back to our desired paths, no matter the hardships we may think we have in front of us. All that happens to us is for our ultimate good.

Once a person has sinned and repeated the sin, he treats it as if it has become permitted. – Arakhin 30b

Habituating oneself to do bad habits or sins, as the quote mentions, automates the action in a way that the next time one will not give it so much thought. Two times already wires the neurons of our brain to the sin or habit in such a way that the awareness of its consequences is diminished, and the gravity unconsciously disregarded as innocuous.

Spiritually talking judgment is not always immediate. Indeed, by the attribute of mercy from G-d it is delayed. The reason is we are left time to consider our actions, to repent, and to go back to the correct path before a heavenly judgment is decreed. It is known from mystic knowledge that G-d did not create the world with strict justice otherwise we would not survive nor a single day. That we do not see its consequences right away should not be a reason to avoid reflection and repentance–or correction, as we may say.

The reality is that bad habits also have consequences. Like before, consequences are not immediate, but develop through time; the sooner we are aware and revert the path of bad habits to good habits, the sooner we will go back to our road to success.

Bad habits are created when repeated, but also destroyed when we will it. That is why repentance requires as a first step the acknowledgment–the awareness–of its gravity, and the sudden realization that we would be better off had we not done the sin. This starts with the will to stop it and not repeating it the next time the triggers come around. Only by truly willing it, it is considered clean in heaven. Once we are determined to change, the mechanisms of change will start gearing up. Stopping bad habits or sins when triggers prompt them and doing good things instead is already easier if we really will it and understand its true nature and where true pleasure is.

> *Through kindness and truth iniquity will be forgiven, if through fear of G-d one turns from evil. When G-d favors a man's ways, even his foes will make peace with him.*
> *(Proverbs 16:6-7)*

Here a mixture of concepts guarantees forgiveness. First kindness and truth, but conditioned on one turning from evil. The best way to turn from evil then is by fearing G-d. In general, forgiveness is given if one truly seeks it. If one desires to walk G-d's path and to depart from evil, there are ways to atone for all past sins.

Being truthful and kind, and understanding the true nature of things help us better to act correctly–and it even prompt us to help others doing so. This is a positive environment where we like ourselves, our friends, and even our foes in turn make peace with us. Such is the power of turning from evil, kindness, and truth.

From a spiritual standpoint it is important to realize that once one walks on the righteous path in general, G-d turns to his favor. There is a way to stop doing bad deeds, bad habits, or bad behaviors and revert to good ones–almost as if the bad ones never existed or had never been done before. Fearing the consequences imposed by G-d, fearing his might, pursuing truth, and acting with kindness is this way.

Repentance is one of the most powerful tools given, because it means that we depart from the sins that we did, and we are not defined by them anymore. If we truly want to walk the right path, the worst parts of the past–even though chastised in case the sins were very big–can be as if we never did them.

Brain-wise we can also expect that the neurons have mechanisms to forget the past and to revert to new behaviors, almost as if they had never been done before–if we train for it.

Overall, the possibility to change must erase from our minds excuses that we cannot change now, or that it is too late. Spiritually and physically the door to change is always open: overall if we reinforce it with fear of G-d; with kindness to all; and with a deep search for truth from reality, and from within ourselves.

He who is slow to anger is better than a strong man, and a master of his passions is better than a conqueror of a city. (Proverbs 16:32)

Anger is a trait that has nothing good. It is very difficult that one never angers. If we cannot avoid it completely, the slower it takes to get angry and the faster we take to be appeased, the better. Anger clouds our minds. It is said that Moses forgot laws when he was in anger. And he did not enter to Israel because in a moment of anger with people's complains about the lack of water, he forgot to bless G-d while hitting the rock to get water, as if he were the source.

Why is being slow to anger better than a strong man? Without anger we can think better. We can assess better the situation and approach it with the maximum rate of success, even in the heat of a moment where anger seems to solve it all. In case we want to lecture somebody we can always fake it, not having it inside of us truly. Decisions taken with anger are very impulsive, and our minds are totally hijacked; the consequences at times are disastrous.

Why mastering our passions is better than a conqueror of a city? The strength needed to master of our passions is higher than the strength needed in what would entail conquering a city. Indeed Samson, a strong warrior that killed a lot of Philistines, lost his physical strength only after he caved to his physical desires [12]. The control of oneself is the key to control many other external avenues. The control of many situations demands a stable mindset under all kinds of duress. That is why indeed the definition of strength is one who conquers his desires.

For though the righteous one may fall seven times, they will arise, but the wicked ones will stumble through evil. (Proverbs 24:16)

That a righteous may fall hints that things do not necessarily succeed on the first try, but must be repeated and trained even for the most noble of causes. Because toil is not taken away for us—we indeed must work for success.

If we have intentions to do righteousness but an evil act was done by a lack of strength, it is not the same than one who goes with markedly evil intentions, where failing means he failed to do his evil plan. If we have good intentions, we will be assisted.

Toiling is part of growth, and failings are steps for the next stage. We must commit to keep working in righteous ways. We must never quit and never despair. Growth is entailed with fallings, and practice improves with mistakes.

That a righteous may fall already shows us that if we fall, it does not mean that we stop being righteous, it means it requires effort and failings. Failing is never an excuse to quit. Falling is part of the process. And a righteous person arises again. Being able to arise again when fallen is markedly and truly a trait of a righteous individual.

What does it mean the wicked will stumble through evil? It means they will stumble with the same very wickedness they use. Evil ways end up stopping one permanently, whereas righteous goals have all the support to be assisted when we fail. We are supported by ourselves, by our environment, and by heaven.

A righteous person eats to satisfy his soul, but the stomach of the wicked will always lack.
(Proverbs 13:25)

Here it is shown the classical drive of man to want more: more seeming physical or material pleasures; more seeming power; or more money even while having it all in spades. We are talking about drives gone unrestrained–usually proper of the wicked.

A righteous person understands that his current situation is his lot–his mission–and truly enjoys it, whereas the wicked does not accept it, no matter what it is. While having it he is always focusing on another lot, and he is not enjoying nor being happy with his current situation to the extent of feeling even miserable–usually due to a distorted perception of reality.

Our missions and paths are naturally endued with pleasure: doing the right thing is naturally endued with pleasure. Only the false believe that doing the right thing is hard, boring, or unpleasant brings us into believing too that doing the wrong thing has any pleasure at all. The stomach gets never satisfied when we believe the fallacies of the wicked. It gets deprived of true physical pleasures–the satisfaction of the soul.

The lacking is real. By focusing all the attention on the stomach, symbolizing the physical and material pleasures in its incorrect form–proper of the wicked–the lacking never ends. When we put our focus on the soul–doing the right thing–then eating and other things become pleasurable and part of a process meant to fulfill a higher purpose; getting energy and pleasures to get to higher goals and pleasures yet: the satisfaction of the soul. The material or physical pleasures are a necessary step to pursue yet higher goals and pleasures: the pleasures of the soul.

> *Only by willfulness is strife fomented; but wisdom is with those who take counsel. Wealth gained by vanity will diminish, but that gathered by hand will increase.*
> *(Proverbs 13:10-11)*

Somebody who willfully wants to cause strife causes it. It does not happen or initiates without a reason. There is a contrast between one who is not fighting for his honor versus one who causes strife to impose his own ideas. The wise listens calmly and hears to take counsel, which even if it is not useful, at least he gets the different points of view to reach to a rightful conclusion.

Wealth gained by vanity–which also means gained in an ill-gotten form, unusually fast, or not worked for–tends to diminish at the end; we can imagine fast earned money like the lottery or any business that earns temporary fast money with a dubious product how it will diminish its earnings at the end, or how they will be spent quite as fast as they are earned.

By contrasts, labored money earned at its right pace not only it will not be diminished, but it will tend to increase or even accumulate a lot later by increasing the business, for instance, or being promoted.

The passage of the Talmud that talks about it [13] tells us that gathered by hand also means gathered little by little–having worked for to increase the wealth. It points out that it talks about physical wealth, but it also applies to the wealth of wisdom. That is, fast gotten wealth or wisdom, without working it or reviewing it, will decrease, whereas done in small chunks and worked for will increase; counsel leads to wisdom which itself tends to make wealth increase.

We can go a little further and apply this concept in our path of growth. If we tend to do a lot of changes in our habits fast, while not repeating them properly, we will tend to lose the progress that we made. It is better to solidify the habits that we do and keep adding them in small amounts first–or for a brief time–so that we feel the progress, work on them, complete them, and let them increase over time.

Poverty and shame befall one who rejects discipline, but he who heeds rebuke will be honored. Lust broken is sweet to the soul, but turning from evil is an abomination to fools. One who walks with the wise, will grow wise, but the companion of fools will be broken. Evil pursues sinners, but the righteous will be rewarded with good. A good person will bequeath to grandchildren, but wealth of a sinner is secreted for a righteous person.
(Proverbs 13:18-22)

Besides poverty rejecting discipline also leads to shame. On the opposite side we have that heeding rebuke, which is paying attention to it and committing to improve, will lead to honored situations. We must not forget that in general also leads to being righteous. Honor is one destiny we could expect for the upright.

It talks in general why the fools do evil. One of the reasons is because lust broken is sweet to the soul, and foolish persons do not want to stop receiving these sweets, at least as per their understanding. Turning from an evil desire is akin to an abomination for fools. The lack of further knowledge prevents them from knowing where real pleasure lies; the real outcomes of the evil acts beyond the perceived gratifications; nor what is missed out while doing them.

When we walk with wise people we grow wise; similarly when we walk with fools we will be broken, that is, our bad habits will enter again. That is why the companions that we frequent is one of the first things to watch out for if we want to head to a good direction regarding who we want to be. Sometimes our own effort is not enough. We must watch out for who we spend time with, since it can ease or hinder greatly our progress.

Evil pursues sinners is a deep concept too. It is known from mystical sources that sins create demons and righteous acts create angels. The more sins, the more demons pushing for more sins. The more good acts, the more angels and the more rewards, opportunities for good acts, and protection we will receive. All this is manifested in the temptations and certain events that seemingly lead to other events fortuitously.

The righteous will be rewarded with good. What does it mean? We do not need to look further. One of the rewards is that the wealth of a good person will pass to grandchildren, whereas the sinner will have his wealth reserved for a righteous one.

This righteous one may not be known by the wicked. An example would be someone who marries the family and ends up enjoying all the wealth.

There is a famous story of a man who received all the wealth of a rich man because he stopped on the road to go to the lavatory, and he became whimsically the only attendant to his funeral. He could only find a private funeral having a lavatory, so he was asked to sign the guest book if he wanted to enter while there was nobody attending really. The story goes that the rich man wrote on his will giving all his riches to the signers of his funeral's guest book. Since the passerby was the only signer, he inherited it all.

My grandmother was a very good righteous person, and my grandfather died long before her. She later reluctantly married a wealthy man who fell in love with her and died shortly after at a very old age, inheriting she half of his wealth. This would serve her to sustain her for the rest of her life. The sons, whatever relation they had with their father, still got inheritance, but not as much as expected.

This and many stories show that good acts attract goodness, and wickedness and evil end up creating events that later come back to hunt the perpetrators.

How much better than fine gold is the acquisition of wisdom, and the acquisition of understanding is choicer than silver! The paved road of the upright is turning from evil; one who keeps his way guards his soul. Pride precedes destruction, and arrogance comes before failure. Better to be lowly of spirit with the humble than to be sharing spoils with the proud. (Proverbs 16:16-19)

Wisdom is one the most powerful tools to achieve what we want to achieve. Every endeavor has its intricacies and knowledge that we need to acquire if we want to do it successfully. Understanding, on the other hand, is being able to see and internalize in our hearts what is the consequence of one action or one wisdom.

Wisdom usually relates to other wisdom, and its details and ramifications is what we would label as understanding. Wisdom is much better than fine gold, for with wisdom one can acquire not only fine gold, but an ultimate understanding of what to reach for and how to reach it. Understanding is by the same token choicer than silver, since it entails the details and intricacies of wisdom at a practical level.

Wisdom and understanding are the power by which we act correctly and we understand our surroundings. I know a real story of a wealthy man who asked for charity because he lost all his money. The couple who gave him charity knew with wisdom that when a person that is used to be wealthy asks for charity, it is proper to give him an amount that is more commensurate with his previous lifestyle. The story goes that after receiving charity to sustain himself, the will of G-d made that, through his previously acquired wisdom, he gained his wealth back, and gave later lifetime sustenance to the couple who sustained him.

Being righteous is a state. Only by the fact that we are walking the path of the upright and we are constantly turning from evil we have our way paved–with less troubles. The key is to keep this way; keep our good ways; change positively if we need so; keep acquiring wisdom; and keep advancing righteously. This way we guard our soul; we guard ourselves from mental and spiritual harm.

The way of the evil also has its signals. When we see pride we may see destruction; when we see arrogance we may see failure. Not always they mean one will fall, but surely if one is to fall he will exhibit these traits before.

It is better to be lowly of spirit with the humble than sharing spoils with the proud, because the proud may enjoy now, but is already giving signs of a harsh fall–and one may be dragged to the same destiny. Being humble on the other hand–or learning it by being lowly of spirit with the humble–has a lot of rewards in store: among them riches, honor, and life. [14]

I am wisdom; I dwell in cleverness; I provide knowledge of designs. Fear of G-d is hatred of evil. I hate pride and haughtiness, the way of evil, and a duplicitous mouth. With me there is counsel and wisdom; I am understanding; with me is might. Through me, kings will reign, and nobles will decree righteousness. Through me officials will rule, and nobles, all who judge righteously. I love those who love me, and those who search for me shall find me. Wealth and honor are with me, great fortune and righteousness. My fruits are better than fine gold, even choice gold, and my produce is choicer than silver. I lead in the path of righteousness, amid the pathways of justice. I have what to bequeath to those who love me, and I shall fill their storehouses.
(Proverbs 8:12-21)

Wisdom includes all wisdom there is, from the knowledge of the sacred, to the knowledge we infer by observing reality. Wisdom is acquired by studying it, discerning its meaning, and finally internalizing it by practicing it or making it our own. As the verse say, loving wisdom is the path to be bequeathed all that is good.

4

Job and Mordechai, always with G-d

Job and Mordechai had both the difficult task of being in very daring situations, yet not deviating not an iota from the exact expected behavior. They were holders of loyalty under duress, and waited patiently for the events to turn around once they did the expected responses. Both are examples of how we must hold our ground when we know all we did is right, and what is coming is a test to keep us rooted–even under the most severe storm.

There was a man in the land of Uz whose name was Job; that man was wholesome and upright, he feared G-d and shunned evil. (Job 1:1)

Job was blessed with wealth and honor. He was the wealthiest man of the East. He had seven sons, three daughters, and lived in peace with his huge wealth. Job is tested later with harsh travails: with the loss his flock; with the death of his children; and with a skin disease. Even after this he never sinned nor uttered blasphemes against

G-d. His case is a case nobody would want to be in, yet at his seventy years of age he emerged successfully. He was given double his previous wealth, he had new seven sons and three daughters–the most beautiful of the land, and he lived a long life even up to living with his fourth generation descendency until he was two-hundred ten years old.

Why did Job have to suffer so much though? He was righteous; he did not sin. So, What was the problem? First, this was a test of faith–to be with G-d in all that happened to him. For some reason at times righteous people suffer and wicked prosper, even though the end is victorious for the righteous.

A lot of commentaries have been written about why he had to suffer–or even if it was just. We never know exactly the heavenly reasons, but sometimes it comes with extra reward we will get in the future; and always suffering is an atonement for something–or in place of other persons. We do have tests, and there is justice. For righteous people justice is more exacting since the reward is enormous, and growth is very perfected.

Now again, Was Job suffering only a test? We know from the Talmud [15] that Job was one of the advisors of Pharaoh when he was deciding if killing all newborn Israelites would be a good idea. While Yitro rejected it, and Balaam agreed upon the idea of killing newborn male Israelites and throwing them to the river, Job stayed silent. The Talmud tells us that he was chastised with suffering for that.

Job, as we can see, was not an Israelite, but a former magician that feared G-d and became very righteous. Yet, he did a big mistake–stay idle while injustice was being made, and justice was also in his hands.

The way of G-d is just, merciful, and good. So, when we see the vicissitudes of life, sometimes we may see that the righteous suffer and the wicked prosper. We do not know exactly what we are judged for, or even if travails come because of previous lives. What we can be sure of is that no good deed goes unrewarded, nor a bad deed unjudged if we do not repent before the judgment is decreed.

In extreme cases if we are very wicked we are paid in "cash" in this world for the little good deeds done; and if we are very righteous we are cleaned up here for the few sins in store, leaving an opposite eternal state for both situations in the other world.

As scriptures say: "I call heaven and earth today to bear witness against you: I have placed life and death before you, blessing and curse; and you shall choose life, so that you will live, you and your offspring." (Deuteronomy 30:19)

As we can see we must keep the righteous path even under our imperfections and stay steadfast to it. This is the way to travers all the difficulties and hardships that we may encounter in anything we do. This way we will choose life in this world, and also in the afterworld: lives full of pleasure, meaning, bounty, growth, and joy.

Then Harbonah, one of the chamberlains in attendance before the king, said, "Furthermore, the gallows which Haman made for Mordechai –who spoke good for the king–is standing in Haman's house; it is fifty cubits high." And the king said, "Hang him on it." (Esther 7:9)

The story of Esther is a story of holocaust. Haman was the Hitler of the time—may their name be erased—and Ahasuerus was king of practically all the known world. It is said in scriptures [16] that only few persons have been ruling practically the whole world. A few of these are Alexander the Great, when Greece was the empire; Salomon, that through political marriages extended his dominion; and Joseph, who made Egypt rich and wide by selling food during a famine to nations in exchange for dominion, silver, and gold. Ahasuerus was king of Persia, and at that time he ruled the entire world.

Haman was the viceroy second only to Ahasuerus and, as Hitler, he was determined to exterminate all Jews. The story of how it unfolds is as simple as, Mordechai, a Jew that was the spiritual leader of the time, did not want to bow down in front of Haman, the viceroy, because Haman carried a necklace with a large idol hanging on his neck.

Haman had an encounter years ago with Mordechai while they were both traveling through the desert. They were both going as lawyers in a case of Jews against Samaritans—Mordechai as defendant of Jews, and Haman of Samaritans. Since the Samaritans feigned wanting to help in the Jewish temple but they were not allowed, they went to court.

Haman ate and drank all his food in the way to the court through the desert, and Mordechai rationed his portion. When Haman started starving to death he begged for Mordechai's food and water, and Mordechai finally accepted reluctantly, but only on the condition that Haman became his slave and accepted to comply if that pledge were ever to be recalled. Since they did not had papyrus available at that time they wrote the pledge on Mordechai's sole. Haman in a way could not force Mordechai to bow down when he was viceroy because he could be reminded that he wrote a legal document back then to be his slave if Mordechai wanted so–so Haman responded then by killing all the Jews.

Years later Haman had it all prepared sending orders to all the cities to kill its Jews at a particular date. Unbeknown to him though Esther, a Jewish woman, had become queen to Ahasuerus; and Mordechai had been her guardian, as she was orphan the same day she was born. Mordechai had also saved Ahasuerus before when people plotted in the gates to kill the king; Mordechai heard about the plot, and warned Ahasuerus about it.

Though the king was saved, he forgot fast about it; and neither he knew that the queen was Jewish. The queen had been chosen by Ahasuerus out of a beauty contest, but he chose her not for her beauty, but for some inexplicable appeal. He had killed the previous queen for disobedience, so Esther was recently installed as queen.

After a three-day communal fasting from all the Jews to revert the decree, the queen revealed that she was Jewish before the execution of the decree, and the king also remembered that Mordechai saved his life when reviewing the court recordings of that year–read because the king could not sleep.

Haman was sentenced to death when Esther disclosed she was Jewish and convinced Ahasuerus that Haman was not having his benefit in mind when planning to execute that huge massacre. She insinuated too that Haman was aiming at his position. And coupled with a later incident where Haman threw himself on top of Esther while requesting for mercy, it settled the suspicions the king was holding on him when he entered and saw all the scene. Ahasureus enraged and Haman was hanged in his gallows along with his ten sons to calm down the king.

This story reveals us how, even in the darkest hour, a salvation comes if people ask for it. In Nazi Germany Jews did not know they were sentenced to die in the camps; yet, when things are gloomy, and the exit seems impossible, there is G-d, the final decider who can change any course of action at any given point–as seen at the end of the war.

Jews had partaken of a whole week of lavish festivals meals with Ahasuerus using ware and sacred vessels that the Babylonians ransomed when the temple was destroyed, and that started the judgement for all they had done. Things have consequences in heaven, and even if not shown immediately, they manifest later in events that may seem unjoined. The realization and immediate request for forgiveness lead by Esther and Mordechai achieved heavenly mercy, and the decree was annulled.

Some say [17] the reason of the decree was they bowed down to Nebuchadnezzar's idols, albeit just pretending because they were being forced, so G-d too pretended that they were going to be killed; public acts of idolatry are forbidden, and to Israel even if death is what ensues [18].

Nazi Germany showed us that in an era of profound disregard for G-d, some could ask for forgiveness and be saved from it all, but if as a people they did not begged for it, it was just not enough. Later all the culprits were hanged and justice ensued. Some say the Nuremberg trials and hangings mirror the hangings of the ten Haman's sons, being reincarnated as the ten Nazis planning the whole holocaust. Indeed one of them shouted the words "Purim Fest 1946!" [19] when hanged–a reference to the festival that commemorates the salvation from Haman by drinking and wearing costumes coupled with the year of their hanging.

People reincarnate in other persons, stories repeat themselves, and villains end up dying at the end of it all. We must be aware that events that happen have a reason, a correction, and consequence–and they also have a way to revert it if we spot our mistakes and ask repentance by doing the right thing and acting good from then on.

Jews were the ones saved here, but in the story of Jonah Nineveh was also going to be chastised if they did not revert the violence that was in their hands. The king of Nineveh was the Pharaoh of the ten plagues of Egypt that survived the splitting of the sea [15], and knew G-d's warnings himself very well: He does not hesitate to execute judgment if not a modicum of regret is shown from all our hearts.

When something happens to us or to a group it is wise to examine what was done wrong spiritually, fix it, and grow. Being righteous under good and under bad is the way to survive and succeed, even if the situation seems as daring as to seemingly be no way to overturn it. A sincere regret is necessary; asking and not changing amounts to nothing. We need commitment from all our hearts. Then is when we really turn the wheels and the ones sentenced for the gallows are promoted as Viceroy, and the ones planning to hang others are hanged with the same gallows that they rose.

Let us always stay sober out of Purim, to get saved from it all, with a clear vision, and with our whole redeemed soul.

How a neuron works

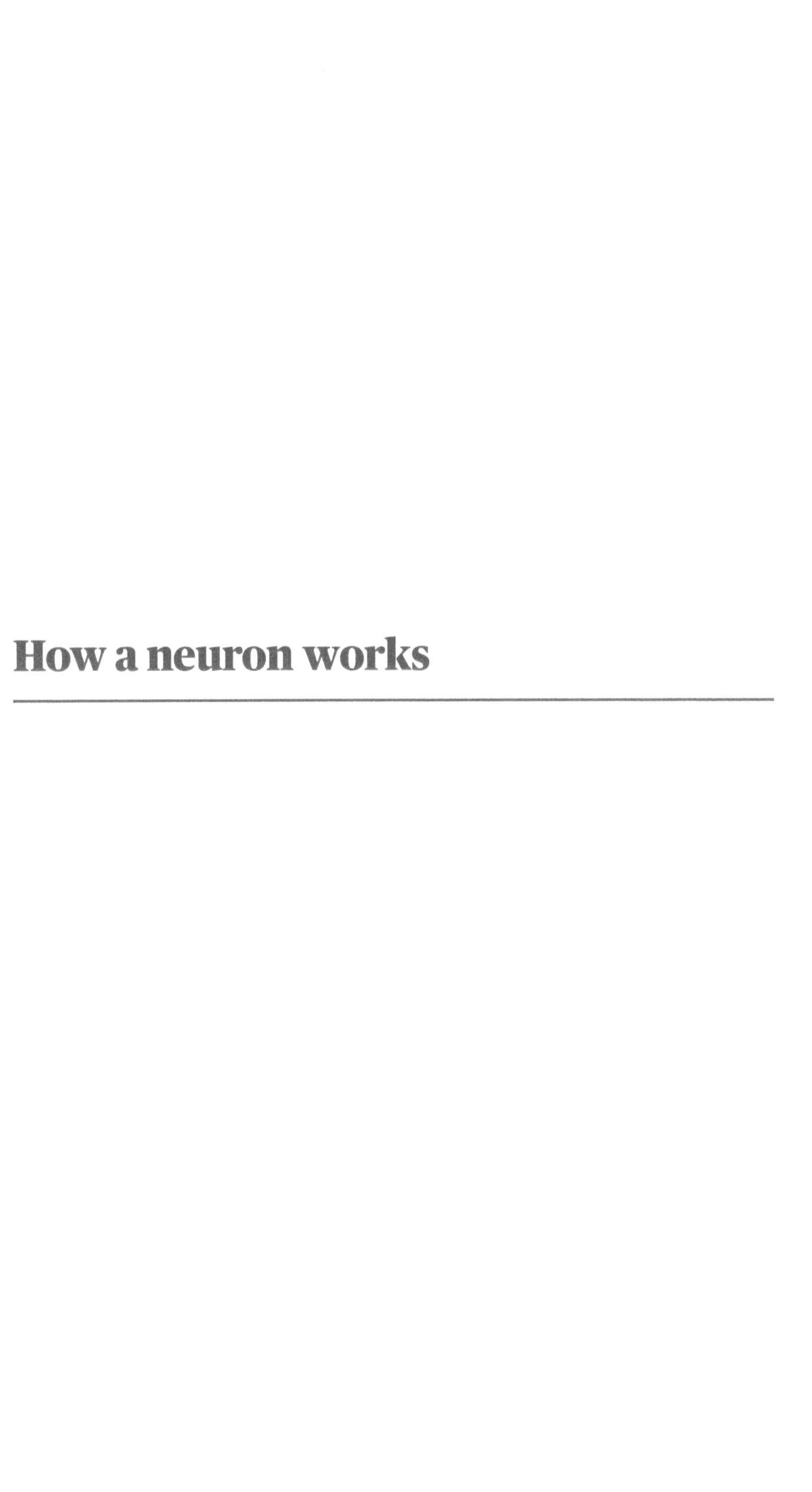

Nowadays we are blessed with a quantity of information and knowledge that we had never seen before. The challenges are equally big. We have a load of distractions that no human being in antiquity had ever needed to deal with. The sheer number of devices that seek our attention and marketing that bombards our brain are unprecedented. To combat this we are equally equipped with the opened gates of wisdom to help us get a better glimpse of how the brain works. The quantity of things that crave our attention, the advanced marketing, and the ever-addictive products and services demand that we understand when our brain is trapped, when our automations take hold and, more importantly of all, how to take the reins back and lead our body to execute what we really want. We will explore and get to know better how to take back this control with the understanding at a neuronal level of how the brain processes, learns, and transforms information. We will explore how a neuron works.

5

Neurons, learning, and traits

The nervous system: where information flows

Even if we may have lofty souls, the reality is that we work in a physical environment, and the physical environment works through time. In this time there are real physical elements and processes that act upon each other and may not change immediately. These processes need to be directed and understood for us to create an outcome, one outcome that is at times way more acceptable and desired than our current ones.

Most of these neuronal processes are stored in the brain. The brain is an organ, the part of our body that holds an intricate network of billions of neurons. The skull holds the brain, but the brain itself is a nut like shaped mass, albeit bigger, of a tissue composed of neuron cells; glia cells to sustain these neurons; a surrounding liquid that protects them; and a series of oxygenated blood vessels that enlivens them and feeds them.

These cellular networks are connected to each other in a length that really expands way more than the brain–it reaches all the ends and most parts of our body. The brain, though, is the central part where most of the electric signals get processed.

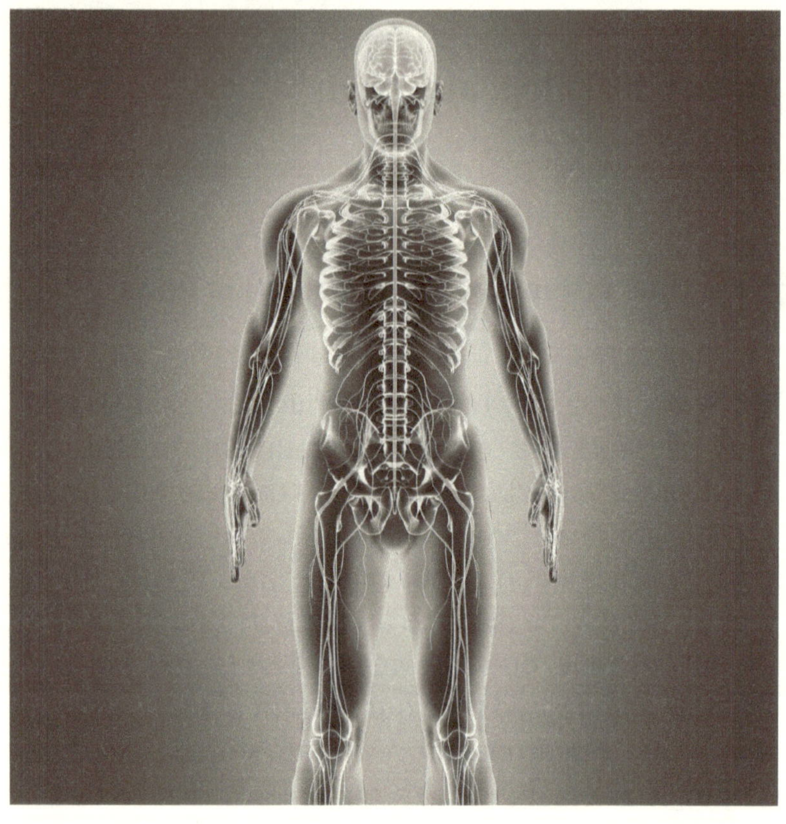

Human nervous system reaching most of the body, and mostly directed by the brain
iStock.com/yodiyim

Next we have neuronal circuits processing in different parts of our body. The heart is one of them, albeit in a lesser degree. It is good that we understand how all this works so we can make better choices that transform these circuits to the shapes that are most advantageous and desirable for our goals.

The brain usually receives stimulus from the sensorial parts of our body. Which are these sensory parts? We have the eyes, the smell, the taste, the audition, and the physical touch. These are mostly the main sensory parts of our body.

The physical touch sensations are located mostly in the surface, close to the skin, with the aid of hairs or bellow skin sensors. There are little receptors that receive different aspects like contact feeling, pressure, temperature, and such.

The eyes sensors are basically receptors for photons that enter to our vision called rods for low light and cones for color. They process photons by, upon hitting the cornea, activating themselves and exciting other neurons in turn. Our vision system can deduce what is the three-dimensional shape of the objects that has in front based on how the photons hit the cornea and reach the receptors.

Light, by the fact of being reflected, holds the information of where objects are located, its measures, speeds, and by way of its color its composition. We know its composition mainly by associating the shapes and colors that we receive with previous knowledge of what the object's composition may be. By looking at the current color and shape with our previous knowledge the brain can rapidly recall what composition it must be formed of.

There is a lot of visual information encoded in the photons—by the energy of the photons, the directions, and the positions that they hit. Surprisingly all of these come just in a small hole in our two eyes. Once these photons reach our eyes, our brain can extract a lot of information from just a few of them, even though only a short number of the photons that are around us reach our retina. Like this we could talk about hearing, smelling, and all the other senses.

Hearing information is processed in a part of the brain dedicated to distinguish and process sounds. The language part of the brain can, out of that information already pre-processed in the ear, recognize words, letters, and understand sentences. It can embed them into a new realm of rules and combinations that are able to understand and talk fluidly any given language–proved we have learned it first. The language words are then automatically associated with vision if they have a physical representation too. Hearing also processes in particular musical sounds, which are mostly linked with feelings–music is a language that speaks directly to the soul. All these parts of the brain entangle with each other then to create, recognize, or recall feelings or concepts that we experience about the world.

The smell information also gets entangled with vision, but surprisingly it gets very much connected with emotions and memories too. The addition of all these sensory information ends up with a wide range of concepts connected with other concepts from different parts of the brain in order to form a final complex perception.

A concept usually ends up being a neuron or group of neurons that are connected to other concepts or lower sensory information. When a group of feelings or thoughts are happening, the neurons associated with them get activated with more electricity than usual. This in turn activates all the neurons that are connected with this concept. This activation of neurons means we are thinking, feeling, or perceiving a concept or group of concepts at that instant of time.

Next we have our heart, that depending on which final understanding was reached or recalled by our brain responds with a palpable reaction–an emotional reaction. How can it be that the heart reacts to the information from the brain? It turns out that not only it reacts, but it shapes our emotional conclusions as well [20]. There is a neuronal connection between the heart and the brain. The heart has a little cluster of neurons that acts as a "mini brain" itself [21]. Though the amygdala is the region of the brain that processes emotions, information or concepts generated in the brain are also received by the heart.

The heart receives concepts and information from the brain and from the body itself, and processes them further to decide what emotional response it should arouse. When finished the heart sends a response to the whole body– including the brain–in the form of hormones [22], neurotransmitters, and other chemical signals.

It is interesting to notice that the heart sends more information to the brain than the amount received by it [23], hinting strongly that the heart may indeed have a bigger role in processing, concluding, and shaping complex emotions than we previously thought.

The heart creates an electric field forty times stronger than the brain [24], suggesting that it may communicate and affect the body and the brain in ways yet not understood by science–and it may even include electromagnetic signals between human beings.

The heart also receives information from other parts of the body. When the heart wants to arouse a response to the whole body in the way of emotions or readiness, it uses a set of chemical reactions that, by way of substances, transmit this information to the necessary parts of the body. Heart and brain synchronize, and in turn generate more substances and reactions till the entire body is in the exact mood that these emotions demand.

The main substances that achieve the desired moods are called hormones. Hormones modify the body exactly as instructed by entering the cells and activating reactions and processes that produce the exact physical state desired for the entire body. There are other substances to arouse emotions like glucose for extra energy or neuronal stimulation for the muscles, but hormones are the ones that play a pivotal role in regulating the entire body to produce a desired emotional response.

On occasions the emotional response must be immediate. Have you ever faced a wild animal and your body suddenly became gazelle-like and started running like there is no tomorrow? The body sometimes must react fast, and the heart, besides the electric signals, is really good at pumping all these substances all at once—or should we say in a heartbeat?

Hormones and other molecules can affect us in a myriad of ways. Our whole body may suddenly be content, or it may be calm. We may become alert, or just become happy. Our heart processes information in its own way, and with the help of the brain it can react and prepare the body fast for whatever it has to be prepared for.

As we can see, the body is affected by what it perceives, what it processes, and what it decides as its final response. Neurons process all this, and the nervous system is where all the information flows: from the senses, to the brain, to the heart, to the body, and some would dare to say that also includes the deepest parts of our souls.

The autonomous system: where autopilot goes on

The brain is the main location where all the electric signals from the neurons are processed. It is where most of the inputs and outputs end up coalescing. We must ask ourselves though, Is all the information exclusively processed in the brain? The answer is no.

There are parts of the body that also hold and process neuronal signals in complex ways yet autonomously. A lot of them are in the vertebral column. These neurons process signals and create complex processes without the need of our conscious activation. The brain has a part in synchronizing them, but they really work on their own.

We usually do nothing consciously when we breathe. Sometimes we can interfere with breathing, but most of the time we just breathe. We are not aware of our breathing intakes. We are not usually aware too when our body gets excited, and the heart changes; or when our whole blood pressure and our alertness also increase.

Sometimes we can interfere consciously if we want to get calmed down. We may interfere with one of the consequences of being excited–like fast breathing. We may decide to inhale and exhale slowly longer volumes of breath to breathe slower, and at that moment create a feedback loop that modifies the outcome and calms us down. Doing this we also affect all its related elements like blood pressure, oxygen level, hormone secretion, pupils' dilation, or even muscles' tension. The heart pumps slower and in turn directs the brain to calm down again. The process is autonomous, but we can interfere consciously. [25]

The digestion is a very complex part that goes very automatic too, yet here we may have less ability to interfere. When we ingest food, the process is complex and involves many elements with transmission of information and signals to control the movement of food and many other things. This process is regulated automatically with some synchronization from the brain, yet a lot of its processes work on their own. The digestion process may learn and adjust to our food types and intake times, yet it is more automatic than others mentioned before.

Walking is another example of automatic process. Our daily routines like walking, running, or even holding the balance in a windy day are mostly automated. When we start walking we are not thinking that we are moving the right foot and the left foot. We just know we are walking, and at times not even that. For instance, we may be looking at the cell phone while not noticing if we are walking or roaming aimlessly in the middle of the street.

It turns out that we function in more automatic modes than we can think of. Our body, for efficiency purposes, is built up with a whole set of patterns and processes that work on their own. Some are created when we are born, like breathing, eating, or holding things. Others are learnt progressively like walking or talking. All in all we would be surprised by how many of our daily activities are controlled by automatic processes.

One of the most outstanding examples of automatic processes is the language. Do we stop to ponder what is the subject or the verb when we speak? Are we making a grammatical analysis every time we want to communicate something? No, we just know how to do that. This happens to the language and many other processes. We can be aware, of course, but a lot of times, once the processes are automated, we do not pay attention. We just want to express something; we just want it to be done. We do not focus on how we are doing it, since it is already pre-recorded. Once pre-recorded, we do it more or less effortlessly.

Learning: a distinctive human trait

Animals are very much pre-programmed when they are born. Most four-legged animals, for example, take very little time to walk when they are born compared to humans. They just wake up on their own and walk. Some walk immediately, others very shortly after. They have some learning, but practically they know how to walk from birth. It is outstanding. After a short period they may just move one foot, and another foot, and there you go, they walk perfectly. It is very difficult to coordinate the movement of a four-legged animal to work well, yet they most do it almost effortlessly from birth.

Computer simulations and robotics show that it is not that simple to program a four-legged animal. The backward legs with the forward legs, how to run, how the backward legs should push the body and the four legs should coordinate their moves. Ants for instance work very differently than four-legged animals, yet they know how to walk from birth and how to coordinate their six legs to achieve many things.

There is a lot of complexity in synchronizing the movements of animals or insects using current computers. We have progressed very slowly in the advancement of legged robots [26]. Nowadays only advances in speed and processing power have made it possible to train neural simulators that learn themselves. For instance, by try and error they acquire the automatic understanding of how or what are the best movements to make a four-legged animal walk; and we are not including the efficiency and speed yet.

Advances in nonlinear optimization to calculate the walking functions and its equilibrium, paired with the powerful processors are the engines of the famous Boston Robotics first military dog. Despite all this, this robot walks slower than an aged person, because it cannot process all the information that involves the simple movement of the legs and balancing of the robot. Interesting enough, by emulating how the brain works, advances in robotics are being made like never before.

History shows us that our best way to make moving machines was to put wheels and to make them turn. By the friction with the floor we would be moving, and by different angles in the front wheels turning. Moving a four-legged animal is nothing short of outstanding. We can pre-record how an animal moves and just try to copy it, but even with our most advanced technology we still cannot equate with the prerecorded processes that most animals already have from birth.

We humans learn, but animals have most of the actions and reactions already programmed when they are born. Animals do have some learning, but upon a more instinctive behavior. When a fawn is born to a deer, for example, it just stands on its own immediately. After a few weeks it moves itself effortlessly. And not only that, but it looks immediately how its mother eats vegetation and imitates what plants to choose when hungry.

When danger comes, most animals have from birth already a fight or flight response that prompts them to attack or to start running. They can remember the danger and avoid it in the future, but they are also programmed to fear certain things on the get-go, like humans do at times. Animals do not improve themselves so to speak. They react to an environment that may force them to acquire certain traits or remember a lot of things, like would be a trained dog, or animals adapting to different environments.

At birth animals have a narrow capacity to learn, and even the neural parts that will handle each type of information in the future is already properly prepared to handle the kind of learning input that will come.

When we are born, we are not totally learned from birth. Indeed, we have to learn how to do a lot of things from scratch. We have to learn how to walk, how to speak, and even how to swim.

Some things, because of the urgency, are not learned. We do not learn how to breathe or how to digest food. Even with breathing though, we still need to learn how to breath when we are on the water, like would be swimming, or how to hold it while going under to make sure we stay alive.

A lot of things must be learned, even basic concepts of our surroundings. Let us take a baby for instance. The fact that when he sees two hands in front of a face and the face is really behind the hands in a three-dimensional world is not so obvious for a newborn child. The human brain learns about the reality that surrounds us anew from birth, from the most fundamental concepts to the more advanced.

The brain, as soon as it keeps learning new concepts, it keeps developing, growing, and maturing. At one point in our lives, though, we see that suddenly subtle aspects of ourselves start to stand out. It turns out that, even though we learn most of the things anew, the way we react to certain things, or some traits of our personalities do have some parts that are hardwired from birth.

• COURAGEOUS • ENERGETIC • CONFIDENT • IMPULSIVE • TEMPERED	• PATIENT • RELIABLE • DETERMINED • SILENT • POSSESSIVE	• ADAPTABLE • COMMUNICATIVE • VERSATILE • INCONSISTENT • CUNNING	• EMOTIONAL • SYMPATHETIC • INTUITIVE • TOUCHY • CLINGING
• GENEROUS • ENTHUSIASTIC • CREATIVE • ARROGANT • BOSSY	• MODEST • METICULOUS • ANALYTICAL • OVERCRITICAL • FUSSY	• TACTFUL • CHARMING • SOCIABLE • INDECISIVE • GULLIBLE	• FORCEFUL • POWERFUL • PASSIONATE • OBSESSIVE • RESENTFUL
• OPTIMIST • PHILOSOPHICAL • HUMOROUS • TACTLESS • RESTLESS	• PRACTICAL • DISCIPLINED • AMBITIOUS • RESERVED • PESSIMIST	• FRIENDLY • LOYAL • HONEST • CONTRARY • DETACHED	• SENSITIVE • IMAGINATIVE • SELFLESS • SECRETIVE • INFLUENCEABLE

Human traits from birth

Some personalities start to be shown at early age one way or another; persons have different personalities even if born with the same parents, in similar environments, or even having almost identical DNA.

Learning: the choice to improve

Every person has fundamental traits that are given at birth; fundamental automatic processes, so to speak, that are pre-programmed from birth; certain thresholds of reaction; certain ways we process information. The personality in its core traits is different for every person. Some persons, though, have similar personalities to other unrelated persons, but they come ingrained mostly at birth.

These fundamental traits we call personality cannot be changed, but we can mold them if needed in some degree. We can choose in which environments to express them, or in which to control them. These types of personalities are the background of our lives, and they are meant to be used so that we do what we are meant to do. They hardly change nor are they meant to change drastically, but must be understood and molded if needed.

We all have certain abilities to do certain things, and it does not matter how many times we train: the excellent performance of something uses both our ingrained abilities coupled with a lot of training at its peak. We have certain abilities in some things, and little or none in others from the outset–though we must push ourselves to know them.

We may know we are good at something because we learn it easily or enjoy doing it. The things we are very good at we like to do, and the bad ones we usually have some degree of distaste. Our personality traits are already predisposed in our brain, and we cannot switch them nor change them for other traits. We can mold them, control them, and choose when to use them, but we have to accept that we operate in a certain way by default.

We can improve our traits to its maximum potential, or make a really good use of them. Whoever we are, this is who we are meant to be, and we must love it.

We must learn anew, though, almost everything: walking, eating with a fork, or whatever we do that requires learning. Reinforcing these abilities can make us very good at something, or just mediocre—even though we are born naturally to outperform others.

When a newborn baby wants to talk, he learns by repeating the same procedure again and again with different variations and corrections that he sees in his mother or environment. For example too when later a kid starts doing some sport, the repetition of the movements makes him more accurate in its execution—probably also observing how others do it. Maybe later in life he starts reading books and the language and his vocabulary is increased too—the ability is improved.

In every aspect that we learn we make effort by repeating it in different variations. The variations are corrected and ingrained till eventually we do all the tasks in an almost pre-programed manner. When finished, the skills are ready to go when the circumstances call for it.

The circumstances that prompt us to execute trained behaviors are called triggers. Our brain and body know how to react to certain given circumstances automatically– and sometimes very fast.

Trained behaviors behave like programs that, given the exact combination of circumstances, start their execution. Our brain, turns out, is full of processes or trained behaviors. Every time we do some simple tasks we must think that probably at one time it was unknown to us and we had to learn it and practice.

Once the brain learns it, it stores how the networks should connect so that we can perform the particular task that it trained to do. This is the initial idea of how the brain works.

The way the network was wired when performing the task is the way it will use when performing it again; sometimes with some improvements based on the last experience, observing others, or even imagining and visualizing its correct execution.

When we are born, our brain is wired and ready to learn new things and new skills. Some things that we learn are already embedded from birth. The ability to wire better or worse in different areas depends on our initial make up and other factors like DNA, environment, etc. Our brain may learn anyway, but we will be better doing some things than others. We have to train nevertheless to do tasks–or to perfect them to our maximum potential.

Emotions: the orchestrators of our body state

Emotions are dealt physically in a more extensive and encompassing fashion than thoughts. Thoughts are sometimes the first processors and triggers of emotions, but once aroused, these emotions usually involve the entire body—and they are very much shaped by the heart, which distributes its signals to the body in different ways.

Emotions usually get associated with concepts generated by our thoughts. Our thoughts may also determine which emotions we associate to certain concepts or certain perceived environment. Emotions are very important to be dealt with. They are mostly shaped by how we store these emotions with certain concepts or group of circumstances.

Some concepts may trigger one type of emotions. Emotions and the environment at the same time may trigger certain concepts. The same concepts may not trigger the same emotions to everybody, and in general, a lot of combinations of concepts get linked with emotions, and in subtle ways.

Emotions have a commonly universal component linked with more vital needs, but even then, it has a very subjective one linked with how we see our environment or how we identify the perceived things to be good or bad.

Some selection of what emotion to display is obtained by associating concepts with an emotion while learning about them, but some reactions may come ingrained from birth in our brains.

Emotions usually are a reaction to things or concepts in a way that takes into account the heart with all the physiological changes it creates. The heart, a physical organ, pumps blood at certain pressures secreting hormones to the whole body and regulating its response, for better or for worst, in one type or another. The way we associate emotions to concepts, by birth, understanding, or will determines how our body will feel as a whole in an almost automatic way to different circumstances.

Like most of the conscious learning we want to do, we can also learn and rewire the emotional reactions differently than what they already are.

Usually there is an innate setup on how we react instinctively and how fast we learn certain things that is given from birth–but we have a conscience and a will that can change some of it if we train for it.

It is very good to understand that we cannot change certain aspects of ourselves, nor try to be the same than another person; but we can mold reactions; train to react slightly different under some concepts; or even channel big emotions into productive ways.

Everybody has its unique DNA, its unique background, and its unique tendency to react to certain things. We have our unique spiritual and physical makeup, but inside this makeup there is content that has also been learned. We all learn to walk, to talk, some in one environment, others in another. Some abilities are common to some cultures, and others are more global. We are born with a disposition to learn, and we must shape our emotions to where we decide it is best.

We ought to shape our feelings, for instance, to focus on the positive side of things and trigger good emotions or effective actions; to judge positive under the doubt to not get distracted unnecessarily and focus on our duties better; to forgive others so that we are not triggered by constant bad emotions of hate or revenge, and unload all these negative triggers from ourselves; to be hopeful that we will succeed so that our entire state is totally focused and ready to perform tasks happily, attentive, and with resolve; to quench any type of anger from ever being activated to have always full control of us and solve situations with cleverness and determination; to accept circumstances given to us with happiness and joy so that we are not consumed by envy; to be full of joy and happiness from any single item and circumstance we have in this life, because all is meant to fulfill our purpose.

Choosing our positive emotions
iStock.com/fizkes

We must learn to control or do most of these things–and more–and even to do them better given our limitations. With training there will be very few setbacks that may shake our core.

6

Actions and reactions

Neurons: a hierarchical way of working

The brain learns processes and the brain stores these processes like a computer program. Different combinations of neurons and its timing of electric impulse can store certain orchestrated movements in our body. The activation of certain orchestrated concepts and feelings function like a computer program–and we are full of these little programs in our bodies.

Our mind and body, in a lesser extent, is composed of patterns of millions and billions of these little programs, mainly stored by the way in which neurons are connected to each other. Some of these processes or programs are more generic and encompass the coordination of different smaller tasks. Others are simple small movements that can be used by lots of generic actions. For instance, we know how to walk, but there are different types of walking. The body knows how to move the feet up, but it can move it in different ways or speeds depending on the goal. The process of walking fast would be a higher level than the process of moving the right foot upwards. Wanting to move fast, though, already determines how fast and slim this movement of moving the right foot up will go.

The vision is maybe one of the best examples of how this hierarchy works. It starts by getting photons from the eyes—the photons themselves are only signs that come at different times from different directions and different energies.

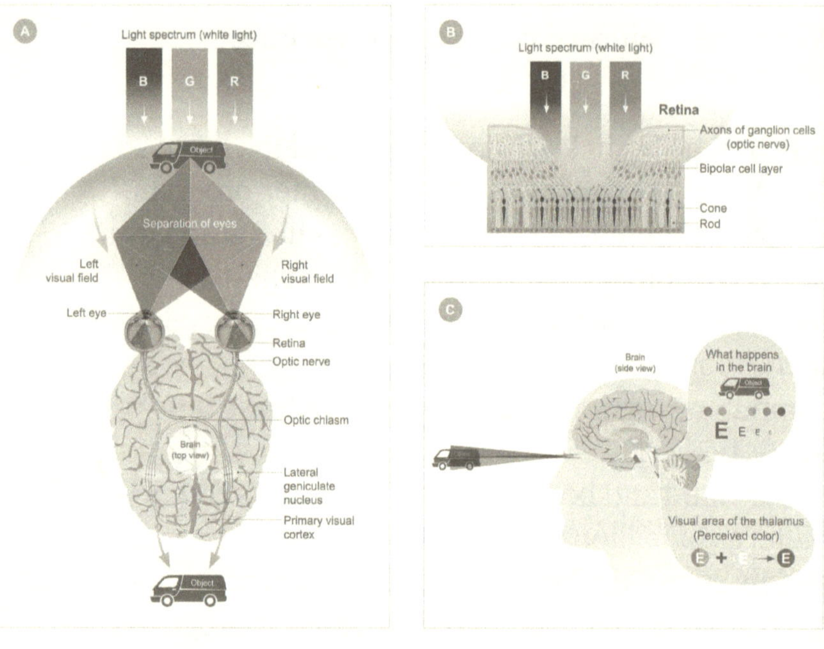

The brain distinguishing a car
iStock.com/Graphic_BKK1979

The photons activating at a certain energy; in a certain position in the eye; from a certain direction; and at a certain time would be the most unprocessed kind of visual signals.

These photons then generate electrical impulses from the photoreceptors to the first layers of the neurons. When all this information joins together in a few neurons, these start to recognize the patterns of different colors and points.

Only when photons come with certain patterns, these neurons would generate an electrical impulse–when recognizing for instance points here or there.

When initial photons activate the neurons that recognize points, these neurons give in turn the information to another layer and they start recognizing lines. These recognized lines would go to another layer yet that would recognize in turn more complex geometrical figures.

Another layer yet would get these geometrical figures and construct some distinguishable objects. Out of these simple objects another layer of neurons would recognize even more complex objects that are composed in turn of these smaller objects–certain wheels, windshields, and chassis would be recognized as a car.

We can see here that the neurons recognize objects by using a layered structure. First they recognize smaller shapes, and out of the previous shapes these signals go to the next neuronal layer of the vision system to recognize yet even more complex structures.

This would be like using a magnifier on our television screen. First we go very close to the screen and distinguish little points. Slightly farther we distinguish lines oriented in different directions. When we put our magnifier a little farther yet we see that these lines form corners. Farther still geometric figures like circles or triangles–maybe of different colors. Even further the figures start having more complex shapes like an object and such. Like this until our brain can recognize what we are seeing in front of our eyes.

Face out of pencil strokes
iStock.com/amoklv

Have you ever seen how a picture caricature is drawn with a pencil? It is just a composition of strokes. One stroke here, one stroke there, and we would finally see a beautiful face just made out of pencil strokes–and even out of color pencil strokes. The strokes would be the layer two of the neurons. We would see lines in different directions and angles. When we join the strokes we would have another level of basic shapes: a corner shape, a round shape, a triangular shape etc. Now, if we put all the shapes together we start having higher level shapes.

What is this round thing with two holes right and left, the upper vertical line in the middle, and a horizontal line laying down? Is this a face? And we would go to the next layer: face recognition. We know it is a face, but which face? In another level up this face could be pale, with the eyes in this position, and the hair, and the cheeks etc. This would the face of such and such.

Face recognition has a whole segment in the brain for itself. Processes or information get reduced very often to a set of lower processes or descriptors, and they are used in conjunction to create higher level concepts. What happens if we see four wheels and a squared like metallic thing? Is that a car? The combination gives away the concept.

Different objects create new concepts–higher concepts still. What would be different cars all together jammed up in a line very close to each other? Are they in a traffic jam? Lower concepts grouped lead to higher concepts. It also goes like this with movement or behavior.

Little behavior movements create low or small processes that when joined together form high level or more complex actions. Have you ever tried driving without learning about the pedals or gears first? These bigger actions encompass all the small processes in a certain order, timing, or strength. Another way of saying it is that an action uses small actions already created and trained in our brain to create a more complex or specific procedure.

Awareness and triggers: molders of our reactions

We can understand now how actions are recorded in our brain. Let us recall similar experiences like when we want to go to work and say to our brain, "All right buddy, I want to go to work." Our brain instructs the body and it in turn starts igniting the car engine. We automatically put the key, the car starts, and we do all the automations to take the car out. We get out of the garage, pick the direction to work, we turn, we go to work, and we repeat these actions almost every day.

Imagine, though, that it were Friday morning and we wanted to go to the mall. Imagine we are not fully aware and we are thinking about something else. We are introducing right now the concept of: being aware. Imagine we were taking the car out of the parking spot and suddenly we turned right whereas the mall was to the left— and we knew it. This is when we realize.

"Oh no! I forgot. This is the way to work. I didn't want to go to work right now!"

What happened here? It happened that it is an act that we repeat and repeat again and again, and it is guiding our body as an automated process. The problem is that we did not want to go to work, but our mind was on other things right then—and we were not paying much attention. We were not aware that the mall is on another route at that moment; our brain was not aware either, so when we started the car and we were getting out, it was the same time of the day, and our body recognized the triggers. It recognized the circumstances where we usually go to work. At that time it executed the process it knew. We did not tell it explicitly to do otherwise, so it just executed what it was used to do. We had not recorded the new process yet–and we were not paying attention to tell it otherwise.

If our body is a store full of automatic things to do, How do we decide which automatic things to store? How do we decide which automatic things not to store? Here is where we use awareness. Awareness is the ability to focus our attention to one specific act or thought. It is where we redirect all the processes to move or execute that certain thing or thought to perform our desired outcome under our supervision.

We could think that, for those more spiritually inclined, awareness has to do with free will–that is the soul. This is the part where, even though we are very much pre-programmed, we may decide to change things. Others would call it consciousness.

Going back to our previous example in the process where we did not want to go to work, and we wanted to go to the mall; let us assume this mall is new and we understand we have never gone before, but we want to go to that mall now. Since we want to go to the mall that we have never gone before, we probably do not need to relearn how to drive, but yes we do need to learn where the mall is. If we look at the map and we see it is at a certain part west of the city, we may need to turn left from the direction we exit the garage. We are aware that we want to go to the mall for whatever reason, and we do not want to go to work now located say on the right side: so we will need to turn left.

Our brain was just about to execute the "go to work" procedure, but we want the "go to the mall" procedure now, so we will need to stop it and execute this new process to not turn right erroneously like before, and to turn left instead. By doing this consciously, and going now to the mall instead of going to work, the next time that it is a Friday morning and we want to go to the mall, we will have it more programed, internalized, and automated. By the mere fact of having done it once it is already more automatic that Friday mornings we may go to the mall– which is left instead of right.

Right now we are learning how to go to the mall for the first time, and we are being aware of the new changes we must do. We are creating a new process: the process of going to the new mall. This is how we create new processes: by making use of our awareness ability; executing the desired actions; and repeating them consciously when the need or occasion arises until they are fully automated.

The body is full of processes that mainly react to whatever situation is right now. Wherever we are it will just execute the closest processes wired that are associated with the current environment. A process is executed when the environment that is associated with that process is being perceived. In case of different candidates it picks the strongest process connected in the brain for that same situation.

If we wake up a Sunday morning without any plan of what we are going to do when we wake up, we will see that our body repeats the same things over and over again–it wakes up in the same way it is used to wake up on Sundays.

If we do not have something pre-planned, it will do whatever it feels like doing–because it has processes already associated with this day of the week, this hour of the week, this environment, and many more details.

If we have from time to time the process or activity of mowing the lawn, for example, when we perceive that the lawn is a little longer on Sundays, then we do activate the process of mowing the lawn when that happens–with all the preparations and actions that it entails. The fact to be a Sunday morning, not having anything special to do, and the lawn being long enough or with weeds, triggers the process of mowing the lawn–if it always grows at the same rate, we "feel" when is about time to mow it.

Some psychologists call these "triggers" or "cues", but it is all the same. Charles Duhigg in his book [27] uses the term cue to identify the circumstances that activates in our brain the unconscious need to execute an action. The brain is full of processes or actions that activate with cues or triggers.

Habits are more commonly mentioned for things that we usually do in our daily schedules, but it is not much different. Some of them are more behavioral than others, so they may be called habits.

Our entire reaction system is made up full of pre-recorded processes or habits. All these processes are called habits, actions, reactions, or even feelings or thoughts. Any chain of events that imply some automated reaction under some circumstance from our body or brain we will call it from now on a process–a neuronal process to be more exact.

Neuronal processes or automations imply a coordinated activity in the brain that actuates in the same or similar way every time it is activated. The neuronal connections that encode a process are kept structurally the same as soon as the process is activated from time to time.

If the process is not activated for a long time, the neuronal connections weaken, and the process ends up being forgotten; we would do it less efficiently next time, or even forget about it completely if doing it entailed some sort of complexity.

If triggers or cues appear and prompt us to do a process, yet we consciously are aware and decide to do another one different instead, then we actively rewire the brain to react differently under the same given circumstances–the old process stops being activated so strongly when the triggers or cues appear, and the new one gets more favored instead. Repeating the new decision consciously enough times when the triggers or cues come around makes us choose eventually and automatically the new process instead of the old.

This is a glimpse of how these processes could be changed, created, or forgotten; and its association with triggers or cues enforced, maintained, or severed. Yet still we should ask ourselves, How do we change them systematically? And most importantly, What do we want them to be changed to? How difficult is to change them? What predisposition does our body have to change these processes? Will it be easy? Will it be hard? What level of success will it have? Are we able to change them at all?

7

Awareness, the driver of the change

Will: the beginning of any conscious choice

The awareness–consciousness–is one of the most important aspects if we really want to change our life. There is nothing that we can change if it does not include an awareness and a will to change. It must start with a desire–a will–for whatever reason it is. Will and pleasure go hand in hand. When deciding to do or start an endeavor or change, the will to do it is the start of the process, and usually it links to an expected pleasure.

The imagined pleasure of an expected gratification is the will that pushes us to do that action. If our knowledge of life already foresees the outcomes, our expected pleasures and wills will aim to the needed actions to get those outcomes. We aim to gain the expected short, middle, and long-lasting gratifications. When aiming at a pleasure, we must be weary that we are not tricked by their counterfeit versions–seeming pleasures that may feel like holding lots of pleasures while really have none, and that lead to no lasting gain while holding us down.

A conscious change always starts with a will, and wills are driven by expected pleasures: from the material, to the relational, personal, or even spiritual.

Lower category pleasures are necessary to reach to higher ones. Not all pleasures live on the same domain. We have the first kind which would be physical or material pleasures; then we have love pleasures; the pleasure of having a meaning in our life–a purpose; the pleasure of the power to create–or creativity; and the highest is the pleasure of connecting with G-d–including higher dimensional realms.

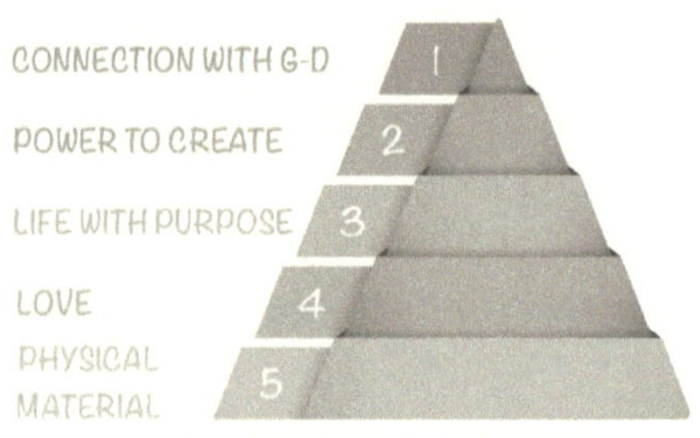

Categories of pleasure

So, do we want immediate pleasures? For what reason? How much? Long lasting pleasures? Deep pleasure from our lives? Of what and to who we want to give? Of where we want to be? Of who we want to become? Of feeling deeply a true connection with G-d? There are different types of wills and pleasures, but they always start with the will related with those pleasures: and we must know first what we really and deeply want the most.

Once the will intervenes, it uses the attention–the conscious mind. When we have determined that we want something and we have associated that will with a certain pleasure, we start visualizing how we can get it and what pleasures it can really give us before deciding if finally pursuing it.

We start by exploring all the possibilities and the paths to reach it. When it kicks our imagination, it becomes very opened ended, full of possibilities. We start visualizing all the ways and things, and how it can be done.

The first step for achieving our will is our brain imagining and foreseeing how it will do that thing, but the awareness is also linked with this process. It is a process where we are being aware of what we want to achieve, of where we are, and where we want to be.

This is the first step of any will; deeper wills could be to ask ourselves what we want to do with our lives. This search of what we want or why we want anything forces us to evaluate all the possibilities and how we could do that: we put that against reality.

What is really in front of us? What are the hardships? How much effort should we exert? Is it possible? Is it not? At times, if it is linked with a deeper will, it may shape who we will become. So, it is best to choose it rightfully.

All this is a process where we are being aware. If we were not being aware–if we did not have free will–we would not want to change anything beyond the immediate perceived pleasures, and deeper processes would not get activated. We would not be higher than animals. The automatic processes would kick in, but left alone they give no growth nor change the processes to reach to higher level goals.

Until there is no motive to change something–we ascertain better the pleasures behind it–we keep doing the same until some awareness comes from us, and we decide to change things–we then do understand why we need to change something and we make it a reality. Until we do not kick that part, the brain will be doing the same all the time.

We must clarify what we are living for; how we can reach there; and what we need to do to fulfill these goals. If we deeply want to change something we must ask ourselves why, explore the pleasures behind it, and dismantle all the false believes–conscious or subconscious–that may be holding us down. We must want it in its fullest form, from our hearts, without fear, and with an unabating trust.

Will creates procedures, its repetition automations

Usually when we want to achieve something or we have the will to change something, what we do and should do is to ask ourselves if this is the correct path, and how we should do it: to analyze all the pros and cons; all the circumstances; what we can do; what we cannot; and what ways we would have to achieve it. Afterwards we would write a plan: write goals of what we want to do and how we could achieve these goals. We should figure out what steps we should do, and set some deadlines for the main milestones.

For instance, if we travel sometimes we may organize our trip for ourselves, family, or friends. When we organize our visit we want to enjoy the visit. We just plan perfectly the hotels, the flights, and if nothing wrong happens–which we would solve it on the spot–everything will end up good.

We have done everything we planned for, we went to the places we had to go, and everything went smooth.

There is a reality here: we had a very big incentive paired with a reward. We wanted to visit all these places where we paid big bucks for. People were also waiting us on those spots–friends and work schedules maybe. At the end mainly everything worked out.

In the middle of it we are us, we have our little habits, and we apply our traits like eating certain things, or maybe doing things our own way. Even if there are unexpected things, we plan, we have goals, and we do them right. We had a strong will and paid a nice amount of attention–we also got exhausted at the end.

When we work we also have schedules. We may leave some hard work for the end, close to the deadlines; it is something natural because of the habits we create, and the less resistance rule. We comply, but one of the reasons we comply is because certain jobs are not the first time we may have done them. And though we may leave the hard work close to the deadlines, we know where the limits are–we learnt them before. This is the average reaction when the procedures are left untouched.

If we need to reach excellency, we train ourselves to do hard tasks first, we get ahead of deadlines, and we preplan good. This needs marked procedures in place that need to be learnt for a while. The extra effort would also need a clear will or an expected pleasure for it. These pleasures are linked usually to higher goals or expected rewards.

We have procedures in place to achieve our goals. We have worked them before because we have been taught in university, at school, or getting trained. We know which procedures to act upon, and which environments is helping to do them.

The military is the same: they have a lot of unexpected things and they are very organized. They have built procedures before. They just activate those procedures, and execute them when in need.

We do have procedures in our daily life; we do have procedures at work; and we do have procedures everywhere. Some are good, some bad, and some bad yet not affecting greatly the outcome, so we may keep them around. Some procedures, though, are very bad and can have big consequences at work, at home, in us, or in others. So, these should be worked out and eradicated first.

Maybe we never advanced where we wanted to advance our career, personal life, and more: and that is because we may have procedures in place that may not be good habits per se or good procedures, and they may be affecting the outcomes—be it that we know it or not.

The military personnel trains to have good habits and to get rid of bad ones, and they change them. At work we train for them; we practice them; we have exams, and if we do not achieve the exams and we fail we must learn how to pass them: we learn how to get a degree or a certificate.

If we are trained for some work or we must learn how to build something, we need to learn how to do these techniques. Whatever craftsmanship we are trained for, we must be trained and prepared for the things that we should do, and the things that we should not. We must make sure that we do the right things if we want our work to succeed: we need to build habits. We must build procedures and that they get ingrained in us.

At home the same, if we are married or living with somebody we need good procedures to keep the expected arrangement in place; to keep peace at home; to live as we desire; and to keep our goals and obligations in check. The same applies to single persons living alone.

All these good procedures have something in common: they are all necessary for a goal that we will. They need to be planned and done, and when repeated a lot of times they become automated. They become a habit: a trained procedure or a habit. They are also paired with a strong expected pleasure and a will to do them. The expected habits need to be well stated and necessary.

Bottom-up approach: plan generic, and train for goals

For some reason sometimes, when we want to do changes–when we want to redirect our life or project in a certain way–things may not work out the way we want. We may do a top-down approach. We may see where the goal is and what things would lead us to that goal. Maybe other things also help us to lead us to that goal, and in a chain reaction by doing all of them we eventually expect to reach that goal. But, what's wrong? Why are we sometimes so much off track? Unexpected things happen in the middle.

The first goals are not achieved, are not aligned–are not perfect. We deviate from our original plan. It does not work out, so we discard the entire plan. We try again a plan B and it may not work out either. We try yet again a plan C and it may also not work out. Eventually we may discard all the plans and get tired of making plans that all together go to nowhere, and we may wonder, What is going on?

Sometimes we face adaptive challenges–not achievable with the existing procedures–and we need new procedures and habits that need to be learned. If we tackle adaptive challenges as if they were technical problems–solvable fast with the existing services, habits, or procedures–we may not obtain what we aim for, because they need new procedures, and they are achieved usually using leadership work: an adaptive leadership that needs to create the necessary changes that will obtain the desired goals [70].

When our goals are complex, and are not solvable by purchasing services, or reusing one or more of the existing procedures or habits, our plans need room to adapt to these changes with new procedures to be learned.

How to do it is we must start having a plan, but we cannot detail all the aspects of the plan. What we must do is a general plan, with its short-term, mid-term, and long-term plans. We can do one detailed plan if we can, but usually the longer term we aim at, the more general plan it needs to be. We must detail less the longer we aim at, and keep iterating the plans–reviewing and planing again–the shorter term they go. We need to know where we should be walking at certain times. We must know what we must be doing, and what actions we should achieve to reach our goals. We always need to know if we are on the right path the longer we go.

When we have a general plan and those general actions in place, What happens next? Then we start changing. But, what things do we need to change? Where do we start? How do we cope with all the myriads of impossible to predict nuances of life, things that block us, and consequences that seem to forever be hindering our plans?

The way to achieve this is by doing a bottom-up approach: we start changing ourselves adequately to achieve our goals. Adequately means changing what needs to be changed for our plans and not changing what does not need to be changed, like for instance habits that are necessary for our environment, or things that we will not be able to change because they are needed for us.

Maybe the way we will succeed was not included in our plan, but the approach of habit making will help us reaching our goals in unexpected ways. Usually goals need a constant work, and this work needs trained procedures to function smoothly: these goals need habits.

James Clear [28] in his book shows us how habit making is a path that usually and unexpectedly leads us to the outcomes we envision. The process of focusing on habits creates an inertia that we carry towards all our goals, and while the goals may be wholesome, the process is equally enjoyable. It can lead us to the expected outcomes–or even to other unexpected outcomes–that are or will be also part of what we are aiming at or we are living for.

Clear shows us how to create habits by exploring how habits form. The most important thing to start forming habits is to really want them, to learn about them, and to keep doing them always with its pleasure and with joy.

The first step is to explore and identify all the habits and routines that we need for our goals to succeed. When identified, we must take note of each of them, and think of its goodness, and how pleasurable is to do them.

Once we have learnt about the good habits and we have seen its benefits, we have to identify them as part of who we really are. We need to see ourselves as non-users of bad habits, and users of all the good habits that we really want. For instance, we could identify us as being healthy eaters, regular exercisers, excellent workers, or anything we want to be from then on.

Habits will start forming by anchoring its execution to a given trigger: be it a time, a location, or stacking themselves to other habits.

We can also make the good habits easier to do by buying equipment, joining the gym, or finding easier ways of doing the good habits. This will start smoothing the process that encourages the good habits to be done easier and with joy.

Naturally we will join people that are congruent with our good habits. In the beginning we can do the good ones for just two minutes or so. Once we are identified with our chosen good habits, we will do them with the intensity that our body demands, the circumstances, or the inspiration that while doing them we spur.

Stephen Guise mentions in his book [29] that in the beginning we may feel more encouraged to do habits at different intensities or variations as we go. Instead of two minutes we can do five minutes, an hour, or more. He recommends having three levels of intensity for habits and three variations, and practice them as we feel with joy.

By being who we want to be we will start creating routines, and unknowingly to us we will repeat them quite often with pleasure and joy as we go. Unknowingly to us we will start projecting a person that will be induced to do the good habits by others, and avoid doing the bad ones to feel good with those we love.

Regarding bad habits–if we still do them–the next and the last time that we do them we must keep in mind how in reality they do not give us anything good at all–nor any pleasure nor any joy. We must identify as non-users of bad habits from the start and from all our hearts.

Naturally what will follow is that we will automatically avoid places, people, or things that carry bad habits. We will not really want certain triggers anymore. The environment around us then will be more conducive to growth.

We will also stop acquiring items or things that lead to the bad habits, and we will avoid people that trigger the bad habits the most. We will perceive the bad habits as something more cumbersome to do, and easier to overcome.

If we keep a daily accounting with a review or diary, talking to us daily, or doing it once a week or so, we will see the progress that we are doing, and if we conform to the plan. Eventually when we desire mastery, by demanding more, we can monitor the habits closer. This way we will do them better, and we will observe its goodness and its rewards.

Start doing the right thing and stop doing the wrong thing lead us to our goals, and it is paramount to produce a change in ourselves. The way this becomes permanent and automatic is not only psychological, but it is embedded in the way the brain works.

Plans are not always as we envision, but doing them is always good to identify the path that we must walk. Reviewing and perfecting them with determination and persistence is the way to go. Only when we know our destination we can always adjust and trace the path we deeply want.

Pleasure and will were our first drivers, awareness is the tool by which we keep modifying and consolidating the change. Neurons remember any good action and any bad action. Only if we choose consciously to do that which we have to do at certain moments, we do modify the connections.

Sometimes we do things that we should not, or we must do things that we do not, so identifying and acting on those moments creates a change that really programs us to automate these responses the next time they come around. By knowing and changing what needs to be changed, unknowingly we will be on the track to our desired goals way sooner than we thought.

Bottom-up approach			
Knowing our end goal, the why of it all, and that it is part of what we are living for	Identifying the milestones—key achievements—and sub-goals that lead us to the end goal	Making an overall general plan of all the steps that will lead us to our desired goals	Keep iterating, planning, and reviewing its short, middle, and long term roads
Identifying the needed habits to have daily and weekly to achieve our goals	Do the habits initially small and immediately after its right time comes	Identifying ourselves as users of good habits and non-users of bad habits for all	Doing our last bad habits and the first good habits knowing where real pleasure goes

Only by wanting it deeply and identifying with it we will be convinced and aligned with our true will, with our true purpose, and with our real goals.

8

Change of connections, the start of the shift

Dopamine, learning, consciousness, and will

We cannot learn how neurons wire themselves without learning a little bit first about dopamine. Dopamine is a hormone that acts on the neurons every time any learning is involved. It is secreted by dopamine neurons, that is, neurons whose function is to create dopamine for other neurons. The way it works is that when dopamine is present neurons start changing and reinforcing its connections in a deeper and more systematical way than usual so that they can remember, so to speak, what connections made the secretion of dopamine. It is almost as if when dopamine appears, in those neurons that it appears, it is telling them that what they did is good—or close to something perceived as good; that they should remember the connections and actions that led to that reward; and that for that they should rewire the same way accordingly to receive the same reward more efficiently in the future.

Dopamine is directly involved with awareness or consciousness [30], and it is when it is secreted that we get awareness and attentiveness to learn and improve. The levels and reserves of dopamine determines how much consciousness learning we will have during the day. It is indeed the lack of dopamine the one that puts us easier into auto mode–even if we desire to keep learning. As soon as we have dopamine we can revert previous habits, automations, and learn new things: we can be aware of what we do and we can improve. Good sleep, good and healthy food, moderate exercise, and having an attitude of joy are the habits that keep dopamine in good levels.

Lack of dopamine neurons and dopamine bad regulated is what happens in Parkinson's disease. Without the needed dopamine it is hard to control body movements. Sometimes the movements or shakings cannot be stopped from its automated chosen mode. On the other hand, some people tend to learn faster or secrete a lot of dopamine while attentive. That would make them good learners, but also prone to addictions.

The more we use it, the more we deplete it for the day. Misusing dopamine for addictive distractions is depleting our own consciousness and tools instead of taking the reins of our decisions, and changing the automations to act the way we want. Dopamine is the main ingredient by which neurons can change from previous connections to the ones we desire.

Dopamine drives learning to acquire an expected pleasure. The main location of dopamine neurons in the brain is close to the region associated with our will. Once we will it, it just informs the neurons implicated in that will to learn to do and execute that which is willed. Pleasure and will are intertwined. Once we perceived something as pleasurable, we will it, and in turn neurons are instructed to get it by learning how to with the use of dopamine.

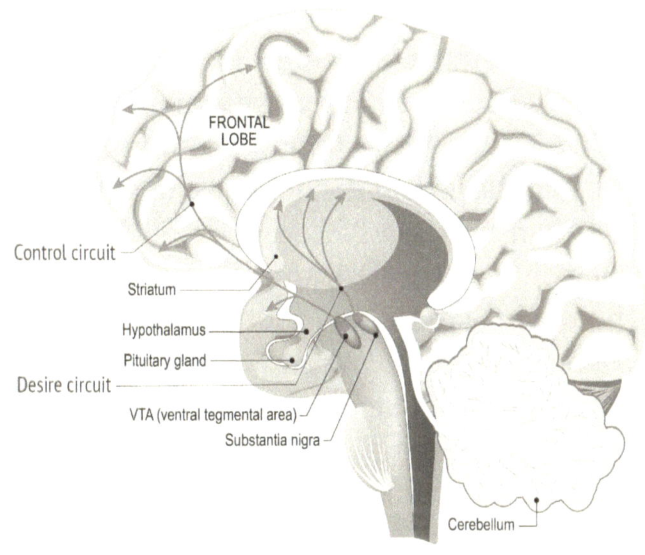

Brain with the two main dopamine circuits or pathways
iStock.com/ttsz

When we give it more thought, we may discern how one pleasure fits into the big scheme of things before willing it. We may discern if it will really give us lasting pleasure now or in the long run. This helps us deciding if we really want or will something before we learn what is necessary to achieve it. We may need to learn an action, by learning what moves to take, or more cognizant, like would be learning to recognize or associate objects or ideas. A strong need and will to do an action directed by dopamine does not mean necessary that we are about to engage in an overly complicated task, which it could, only that we are very determined and driven to do that action with success.

Daniel Z. Lieberman and Michael E. Long show in their book [31] that dopamine is exclusively for learning. Once we learn how to get something, dopamine is not so dominant. It returns to its baseline levels and the hormones that do give pleasure like oxytocin, serotonin, or endorphins kick in, showing us that the goal of dopamine is more learning to get a reward than the reward itself.

It is our will with the expected, and at times imagined pleasures who drives learning and a lot of our actions, not the real pleasures themselves. We could say that our imagination and expected outcomes is what drive our actions and learning. We may have felt the pleasure before, but if the next time is uncertain as to what degree or form this pleasure will take, the brain imagines exactly what it expects without knowing really its type or its form.

Sometimes we may fail in identifying what is really pleasurable and we may become addicted to something that is really not giving pleasure. That is why one of the two circuits with most abundant dopamine generating neurons passes through the regions in the brain that imagines, foresees, calculates, and predicts; so that it aims at the most accurate expected reward in reality possible [30].

Thinking things through and being aware of reality and the consequences of our actions already makes us perceive a pleasure as what it really is; be it a need pleasure for getting higher pleasures; a good meaningful one and looked for from our souls; or simply a false mirage that leads to pain or emptiness in the long run.

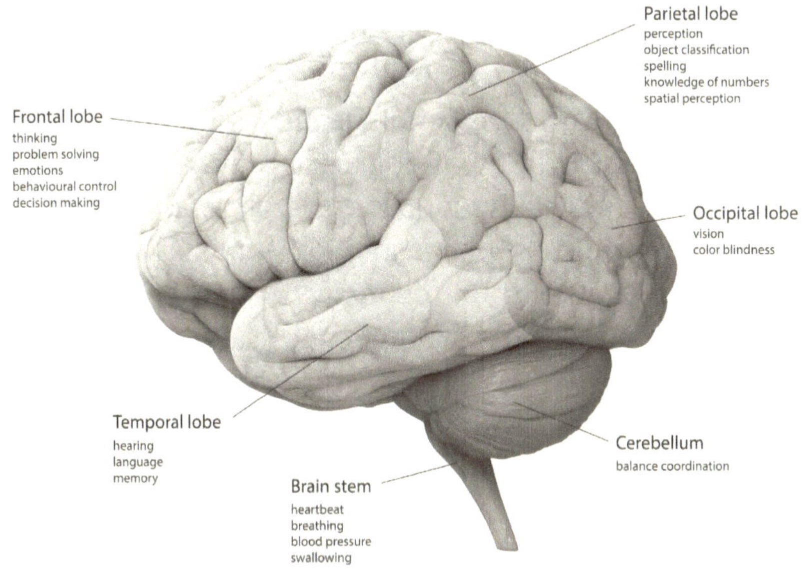

Frontal lobe region traversed by dopamine, where thinking and prediction determine if something will give us pleasure
iStock.com/Martin Broz

A strong will and an understanding of what we perceive as pleasurable are really what drive this learning and push us to achieve something. It is our duty to study wisdom and to understand what is really good and pleasurable now and in the future so we are not fooled by a misguided imagination picturing ideas of what something may indulge us with.

This need for learning to get a reward is what drives compulsive addictive behaviors when the reward is not satiating and the use of dopamine is extreme. Examples are: behavioral addictions like gambling, stealing, casual sex, or other destructive things; brain altering substances like drugs from leaves, pills, or other means; coffee, sugar, alcohol, and some excitant drinks; ultra-processed addictive foods with sugars, non-healthy oils, and processed grains in fast-food or packaged meals; online sex, online gambling, online shopping–overall when it really is beyond our means; over-consumption of media like games, television, social-media, or too many news feeds; a myriad of items of supposed entertainment all available now at our finger-tips.

The amount of ready-to-consume things nowadays that sell themselves as pleasures and we may use as an escape is unprecedented. The question we must ask ourselves is, Are they real useful pleasures what we seek at times? Or are they bereft of any pleasure yet desired for the escape they provide while reaching to them? It is good to stop worrying about things once we have done all we could to solve them. Examples of positive things to calm us down are prayer, meditation, or healthy activities that may help us stay positive and joyful with the worries we may have [32].

When we reach for false pleasures to distract us from our problems, we face the dangers of falling into bigger holes. The problem is that the available quantity and the power of crafted realities that exist nowadays create an escalation of adaptation from the neurons that, once we have achieved a supposed pleasure, since it is not a real pleasure, the neurons keep pushing endlessly for more supposed pleasures to feel satisfied without much success.

When receiving a temporal dose of dopamine for a false believe that we are closer to a pleasure, the lack of the real pleasure in addictions ignites again the dopamine creation process in such a way that, even though we may try with higher intensity, the real pleasure that we seek never truly comes. The only relief we feel is stopping the cravings from bothering us temporally. All this then produces such an abnormal use of dopamine that we do escape from reality indeed–but not to a healthy one.

Digital escapes without pleasure available nowadays
iStock.com/DrAfter123

Being satisfied is normal when anything we want to achieve is learned to be obtained and we know how to get it fast from then on. We worked, we learned, we got it, we are satisfied, and we know how to get it without effort the next time we need this pleasure.

Gaming, for instance, with their feedback data, their imaginary worlds, and the endless learning to get digital rewards moves a humongous billionaire industry of players perceiving the game as a pleasurable reality, while the reality cannot be further from the truth.

Smoking is an example that I have avoided always since I was a child. Not only smoking is not a pleasurable thing to do, but it is indeed disgusting. I still remember the countless times that I threw up in the car because of this horrendous smell, and the enclosed drowsy set up proper of a moving car. The awareness of the addictive power of smoking was intense as a child. It made it clear to me that smoking was something to avoid–because I would not know if I would ever get out if I ever tried it once.

I tried smoking once, a cigarette puff, to light the cigarette only, and it was totally to get out from a circumstantial situation. I still hate it, and I did it with disdain. Once it was lit, I just let it burn discreetly between my fingers till it consumed itself, while I was throwing away the cigarette ash flicking my thumb against the filter, as an avid smoker would skillfully do.

The next day I craved for one more cigarette–just to relive the thought of a seemingly pleasurable feeling of where I was when I took it. I did not. And I feared then that it would bother me, but it was just that time. I have never craved nor taken any cigarette puff ever more. I had witnessed its destruction and addiction all too close during my youth. If something, I still have respect for its power to devour countless people of all ages, sex, denominations, and societal strata.

So, What is so bad about smoking? Is it its cancerous nature? Sure, that is clearly one of the reasons, but, What does it do to our brain besides needing to spend money and needing to smoke it just when the cravings demand it? Does it give any pleasure taking these horrendous smokes into our lungs? As a passive smoker all my youth I can say no. Definitely it is the opposite of pleasurable. Why would people keep smoking then with the hideous images that they show on cigarette boxes around the world showing its consequences, or knowing the fact that cigarettes kill half of its users if not quitting on time? [33]

Who is the culprit? The culprit is nicotine–an insecticide.

Nicotine is the main malicious component of cigarettes. Nicotine itself does not give any pleasure to the brain. What nicotine does, besides destroying lots of parts of the body by associating itself with cigarettes' chemicals and making them one of the leading causes of premature death in the world, is causing a boost in the brain of exaggerated amounts of dopamine. This creates a disfunction in learning tasks that promotes the more impulsive decision making versus the more explorative ones [34], and it is the main cause of addiction. It robs us from our consciousness; or better said it depletes its reservoir in place of focusing on haphazardly chosen moments determined by the time one choses to smoke, or the things one decides to do before or during smoking.

Dopamine itself does not give any pleasure. Indeed it is the opposite. When there is a temporal increase of dopamine, there is immediately after a big depletion that the body needs to replenish again to rebalance its normal levels. To replenish it a feeling of unease ensues. This feeling prompts us to perform the action that will replenish dopamine to normal levels. This action is usually the one that gets the expected reward whose will to achieve generated the initial high and later craving in the first place. In the case of cigarettes, nicotine starts the cravings, and we would need to consume it again to generate enough dopamine and replenish the void generated by it to feel normal again—in this case without pleasure, since beyond stopping the cravings, nicotine gives none instead.

Any action or objective that we want to achieve and whose way to get it is not yet totally automated in our brains generates a process of learning that starts secreting dopamine. It does it as soon as the body decides or wants to get something. This dopamine then is depleted from its normal amounts creating that feeling of unease and craving that pushes us to perform a task. Usually, when we achieve the objective pleasure hormones are released, and dopamine is secreted back to its normal levels, calming us down and making us feel satisfied and accomplished.

Nicotine from the cigarettes or vaping devices moreover potentiates initially the feeling of satisfaction, because it ignites artificially the generation of dopamine. Initially it seems as if we got over satisfied and more attentive to everything. It just uses more dopamine for the same task— that is, higher depletion, and higher amounts needed to rebalance the dopamine levels again making us feel as if we achieved something humongous. The problem is that the body notices this big overuse, and to compensate it decides from then on to start relying on the signal from nicotine to start generating dopamine, and less in the natural mechanisms of our bodies to decide when a good time is to secrete dopamine. This shift of the trigger to generate dopamine from the body to the nicotine is done so that normal amounts of dopamine are always generated.

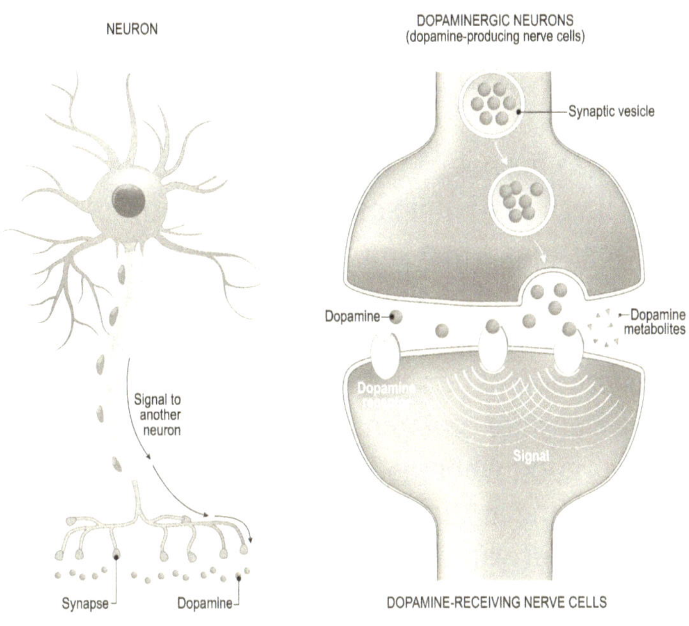

Dopamine secreting neurons being activated
iStock.com/ttsz

When we stop smoking then our bodies are not able to generate dopamine as before, because the signals to generate dopamine from nicotine suddenly disappear. Then a feeling of uneasiness and discomfort ensues unless the cessation is long enough to let the body generate dopamine by itself again. In the meantime everything may seem a little less interesting, and we may have feelings of uneasy and craving–until we wait a month, or take another cigarette or vaping's puff. Smoking initially increases the level of dopamine more than what our body would naturally generate. So, when I smoked that small amount once it did not give me pleasure, it just associated the circumstance I was in as something desirable to repeat–and that does not necessary involve any pleasurable activity at all.

Allen Carr in his book [35] with the world-renowned EasyWay® method to quit smoking shows how pleasure is totally nonexistent when smoking. He also shows how all the justifications and feelings a smoker has about the goodness of a cigarette are complete fallacies created by the artificial secretion of dopamine made at the times chosen to smoke a cigarette or vaping device: dopamine is telling something is good whereas, since the secretion of dopamine is done artificially, a smoker ends up convinced that a cigarette or vaping device is giving lots of good benefits that do not really exist. Allen Carr's concepts applies to smoking and any addiction that uses dopamine–which are all.

It is our responsibility to learn the truth and to stop our justifications so that we can generate dopamine at its normal levels. When recommending a friend to buy Allen Carr's book to quit smoking he said he only vaped instead, and I only received wonders about vaping. The benefits of vaping in Carr's book are explained with a blank page.

Smokers usually are known to smoke after pleasurable meals or other pleasurable situations, indicating that usually the lower capacity to create dopamine from their system is not filling naturally the depletion or cravings created before a casual pleasurable activity. The shot of nicotine that triggers the generation of dopamine compensates the natural inability of the body to create dopamine as before, and that helps to keep that feeling of accomplishment after a pleasurable thing or activity is obtained.

The body relies on the smoker to ignite the generation of dopamine at times instead of doing it all by itself. The dangers as we can imagine are obvious: one cigarette done sporadically forces our dopamine neurons to generate dopamine, whether we are learning or whatever we are doing. The brain will crave for more nicotine if accustomed to it because it starts associating the nicotine as the dopamine generating element instead of its natural processes. The more nicotine, the more the production of dopamine is shifted to the cigarette–that is to nicotine. And that dictates the body when to generate dopamine from then on.

When learning or doing activities of learning that expect a reward, the body itself will not be enough to supply the missing dopamine, so feelings of not fulfilled expectations are expected overall close to the accustomed smoking times. This would explain the attitude of indifference proper a smoker–as if the world does not excite him–because indeed his natural dopamine production is hampered, and only when taking nicotine–or quitting–are his baseline levels restored. This would apply to all addictions including other activities, or harder drugs too.

Alcoholic drinks, for instance, promote the generation of dopamine; being alcohol the main addictive component. The reactions to the brain are inhibitory in nature, but the illusion that one is doing great and feeling skillful even when lousy and impaired when consuming too much alcohol is achieved by the secretion of dopamine induced by alcohol. The dopamine dependance mechanism is the same.

An addict to anything is more prone to get addicted to other myriad of things. The lack of the body to generate dopamine favors high dopamine generating activities in place of normal ones. The addict is prone to start over-generating dopamine via other addictive activities because the dopamine production is distorted by the addiction.

The smoker is prone then to favor, for instance, currently offered illusionary mind-swindling activities with make-believe never-ending non-real pleasures, or ever increasing conscience-blocking learning challenges that are difficult to fulfill and are nowadays so highly available as scapegoats. He is also prone to use similar stimulants like would be alcohol; brain altering plants or mushrooms; high amounts of ultra-processed foods; high intake of mild, but very common drugs; or even harder and illegal drugs. Dopamine generating addictive activities and substances are now offered in spades.

Cigarettes are also smoked in times of distress and anxiety. This is craved because the body secrets high doses of dopamine levels when one feels the pleasure of pain—or better said, the after-pain relief. Painful moments deplete dopamine, and after these stressful situations the body naturally secretes pain relieving hormones that in turn secrete and restore dopamine to remember it as good.

The smoker has less natural capacity to secrete dopamine hormones, and needs to artificially secrete them with a cigarette instead. The misuse of dopamine neurons makes a smoker not able to reach the equilibrium baseline nor feel really relieved on its own. It is not that the cigarette causes relieve, but it is the one that robs the smoker from the natural relieving mechanisms, and that creates this exaggerated discomfort and stress to begin with.

Today I saw a relative. I asked him.

"You look happy. How are you doing?"

"Excellent! You know David, I regained my normal weight! You remember how hard was for me to gain weight, right?"

"But don't you prefer to be slim like before?"

"No David. Come on! You know how strong I was before. Now I have finally recovered my true weight!"

"But did you eat healthy?"

"Of course, the way to gain muscle is eating healthy, not snacks. You know that. Look at these legs!"

"Do you feel more energetic now?"

"Yes. Now I have energy, lots of it. Before I was always tired. I could lay in the sofa all day. It was horrible. My friends think that I am taking drugs pills or something. Ha, ha, ha!"

"I think you know when you were able to gain weight again."–I said.

"No, I don't. When I left my latest relationship?"

"No. Are you still smoking?"

"No, I quitted eight months ago from that ****. Wait a minute... Oh, now I know!! The cigarettes, right?! It's true. I started gaining back again my own weight when I stopped smoking! Wow, how true! I did not even remember that I used to take that ****."

The secretion of dopamine is not only unnaturally triggered by substances like sugar, caffeine, alcohol, or any addictive drug. Activities that are prone to demand a lot of attention and interaction may also end up producing a lot of dopamine when interacting with them. Digital addictions, money gambling, shopping, risky activities, or any other demanding habit that we may revert to as an escape are prone to use up a lot of our dopamine reserves.

Even before we perform dopamine demanding activities, the cravings and our habituations already procure a reservoir of dopamine for them. During normal life activities the body then uses less dopamine to be ready for the more demanding ones. Practicing them at night or even during weekends may seem a better option than during the day, but because of the anticipation, they will still affect greatly the dopamine levels during the week.

The attention to life itself gets diminished with so many artificial interactions with dopamine–and in a high degree. Dopamine is a powerful attention demanding hormone. Only by quitting all addictive activities and recovering the normal levels of baseline dopamine, we do get excited about the world again, and regain the necessary attention to it, to our loved ones, and to ourselves.

Even something as healthy as doing sports can become addictive and detrimental when moved to the extreme. I am a witness of that when I almost died when I was young by overexercising during some days, culminating in a drowning in a swimming pool that needed cardiopulmonary resuscitation from a nearby doctor. I often used to hear also comments on the locker rooms about burnout ankles and countless illnesses coming out from too much exercise.

Pain in the extreme later needs to be regulated by secreting pleasurable hormones–and we can get addicted to this process and perceive it consciously as good too. If we use it as an escape, we should watch out, because if we will it, dopamine makes sure that we get there, and we learn the most dangerous sports till it is too late to unlearn them–because we could be no more.

The fierce power of dopamine should be used to grasp our real wills: our deepest soul desires of who and where we want to be in life. It is the mere will and confidence that we will get what we envision what drives us to learn the unthinkable, achieve the unimaginable, and pushes as to do and perfect ourselves till all our goals and steps have succeeded. They lead us to our expected higher reward, even if in the meantime we only see the middle steps, the immediate achievements, or even pain. Dopamine is like the substance that pushes our neurons to perfect us, and demands from us that we do what we do as best as we can.

Dopamine, in summary, is the main neurotransmitter known to regulate learning in neurons, and it is certainly the hormone that pushes us to do our desired wills. When we want to learn something, it secretes a little amount just by imagining the expected reward, be it short termed or long termed. Dopamine is always being secreted at a baseline level, and the body tries to regulate it to its normal levels when it varies from its normal amount.

We are always learning, and in every little action that we do the brain readjusts or keeps learning and wiring if needed to maximize its expected pleasure: be it because it is already mostly automated and just perfecting it; or that we are willing something new. Usually when in learning mode, it requires attention in some degree–though at times it is so fast that it just uses very little of our attention span, like would be fast mental decisions, or the movement of our eyes. Once these little variations of dopamine levels go back to normal our attention is not required anymore: this is a homeostatic process.

Homeostasis studies the regulation of the body to maintain stability. I have been working as a researcher and developer in the extensive team that builds machines that detect these invariances for close to six years now. These machines are used worldwide, and the company that builds them is the industry leader in the diagnosis in this field.

Dr. Anna Lembke explains in her book [29] how dopamine, when it is secreted for learning, spikes and later goes down below its baseline level shortly after to get our attention so that we learn something. This creates a pain and a craving that is needed, and pushes us to do and achieve tasks and their associated rewards. When completed successfully we get pleasurable hormones, and a new boost of dopamine to regain its normal baseline levels.

Neuronal learning: spike together, wire together

Dopamine activates the learning mechanisms in the neurons, But how do neurons learn really? The main simple way neurons learn and rewire is that if neurons spike together, they wire together. Ramon y Cajal was one of the first neuroscientists to study neurons, and his life work gave rise to the discovery that a neuron is the main cell and mechanism by which information is transmitted, stored, and learned in the brain. Later all the different variations and specifications of how neurons learn or spike have better pinpointed the diverse ways neurons work, but this is still the main mechanism of them all.

Besides transmitting information, when neurons spike together at the same time to the target neuron, they also learn. The connections to the target neuron get reinforced. This group of neurons that achieved a spike will be connected strongly next time. The following time that they will transmit electricity it will be in an easier way.

The presence of dopamine through dopamine neurons makes neurons learn even deeper: the time window to consider if neurons spiked together is increased; the reinforcement of the connections is strengthened; and neurons involved in the task being learned are more pin-pointedly selected with dopamine pathways. [36]

We can see now how the concept easier execution with repetitions starts at a neurological level. The group of neurons that spike strongly enough to create a spike to the target neuron connect and get wired strongly, making the target neuron remember the neurons that made it spike. That means that when this same group is activated at the same time, they will transmit more electricity to the neuron. The combination will most probably make the target neuron spike, because now they are more efficient together each time. The neurons that achieved that spike will wire. These neurons may include actions that were around the spike, like feelings, thoughts, or ideas had during the spike. Consequently they will be retrieved or perceived later more automatically together, because they do create a spike.

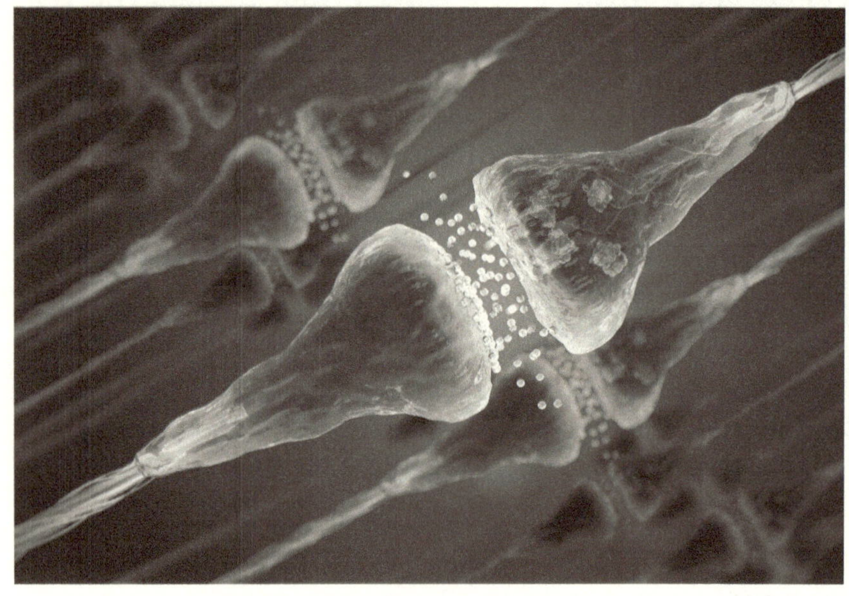

Neurons' synapses transmitting electricity at the same time
iStock.com/cosmin4000

Neurons usually process a lot of information, and they have the ability to encode that information in very few spikes and connections. They not only use space, but also timing. When we see networks spiking, the same neuron that is used to activate one thing is used to activate another thing. We may have even competing actions trying to be activated by the same trigger. How an action will win over the other is something fascinating–maybe because of its simplicity.

The way one action or process is preferred to any other is by a constant change of neuronal connections called reinforcement. First neurons learn to recognize a trigger–an ideal moment to do an action or process–and then the actions that are connected to this trigger will get activated when this trigger appears. In case of conflict the first to activate inhibits the other options. One option chosen consciously then is able to inhibit the other options changing something we were used to do for something else –not without some effort and tiredness at times.

The mechanism a process uses to recognize objects is also used to recognize environmental triggers–or cues–that will evoke reactions from our part. Instead of recognizing objects, though, it recognizes the environment that must trigger the start of an activity. If an environment happens and we do not do an expected action or activity, or choose willingly to do something different of what we feel like doing, then the connection between the trigger environment and the old action is weakened or forgotten.

Knowing how neurons learn in general helps us better understand how repetition reinforces certain patterns in the environment with certain behaviors. We will repeat the desired behaviors in the future unconsciously, or better said, automatically–in a very inclined drive to do so without much thinking.

Any meaningful change will need effort and awareness to change it in the beginning. That is why the energy involved is limited, and we need to keep changing one step at a time. Neurons learn when higher doses of dopamine appear, rewiring and achieving an objective. If we have used up most of the dopamine, neurons do not receive later that much dopamine, and they do not learn as efficiently; choosing the automatic response instead, and making changes more difficult till we sleep, eat, or recover ourselves.

But how do neurons learn to recognize objects? Let us imagine we have never encountered the concept of a car before; that we receive then images, one after another, but we have no idea which of them is a car. If we remember the concept of descriptors, our eyes start by looking at photons, then the neurons recognize them as points with more contrast than the rest, then they recognize lines, shapes, forms, and finally objects with meaning and in different colors. All is the same image but it is processed and recognized fast in this hierarchical fashion.

Let us say we do not know yet, neither have we been briefed of what a car is, nor how it looks like, nor even for what it is for. Let us imagine that there is somebody who tells us.

"Hey, you see! This is a car."

Just when we were looking at a car. And that our brain did not have the concept of a car yet, but we recognize shapes, forms, or objects that may compose a car. Then somewhere in our brain there would be some freed network of neurons–or even a single neuron–just ready to learn. Let us imagine it is still not used for too many things, or even if used for a few things its use is so little that now it will be recycled. Who knows, maybe it was already distinguishing that weird object before, only it did not know it was a car, nor what it was for. Now for sure it will be used to know what a car is.

This is how a neuron associates the features of a car with the concept of car. When we are looking at a car and they tell us this is a car.

"See remember this is a car."

First, we want to learn and expect the benefits and pleasures from it, so our brain will change those neurons with which it wants to learn this concept with the help of dopamine. Neurons will rewire efficiently to match the situation where we were told that an image was a car, and the next time we see an image of a car the neurons will deduce it is a car. By the visual descriptors that neurons choose to distinguish what a car is they will know if what we see is a car or not.

As we explained, dopamine in the brain is secreted by dopamine neurons, and it is involved with learning. Every time somebody told us something was a car, we had the pleasure and the drive for some reason to remember that, indeed, what was shown was a car. So, the connections changes to achieve that objective. The will and awareness have be active, so that when we recognize a car we get some benefit of learning what a car is.

In this case we would get a new secretion of dopamine surpassing its normal baseline levels when we successfully recognize a car. When the dopamine is high, it instructs the neuronal connections to remember the exact combination of connections that allowed this successful situation by reinforcing them. When finished the neurons go back to its baseline levels of dopamine. This new neuronal connection that has learnt to recognize cars can then be reused the next time that this task comes around without using extra dopamine–nor our attention–making it more automatic.

The benefit of learning correctly is the secretion of pleasurable hormones after a shot of dopamine when the car is recognized as expected to remember what we did good, and to rebalance the dopamine path of the neurons that are learning this task until another car comes along. When we start recognizing cars consistently it uses less dopamine the next time, because we are learning correctly, and we do not need to rewire neurons so much anymore.

While learning, though, How do neurons modify the connections to learn what a car is? When we are looking at a car for the first time, our brain may not know yet what a car is; but it may know what a wheel is, what a box is, what metal is, what square is, and what round is. Now, while learning and watching a car, the neurons that codify four wheels holding a big chunk of metal box would start spiking. Maybe there is somebody in the car holding the driving wheel, so the neuron that codifies that round shape thing with a person in there starts spiking too. Little details that we may not be aware also start spiking. The neurons that codify them start spiking.

We may recognize now that that image is a car but, What is the concept of a car? That is one car but, How do we know the other object is also a car? Is being shown one car enough?

If we learn only visually, we will be shown different cars with different variations. Over time the appearance of rubber wheels, proportion of the car, or the chassis of the car will always spike when we see a car. Our brain will identify that when it sees an object with all these characteristics, it is a car, because all of them will spike together to the car neuron telling us this is a car.

The neurons that correspond to the objects that compose a car in our example were always spiking together when a car was seen, so the car neuron, little by little, reinforced the connections of all the properties that identify a car. The dopamine present in the neurons heightens the process of reinforcing its connections when a successful recognition happens. Next time that we see a car and all car properties spike, the car neuron will be sensitive to them, and it will spike too, informing us that that it is a car indeed, and also telling other neurons that we are thinking about a car, or looking at a car.

The things that are spiking every single time we see a car may be the four black wheels made out of rubber in that disposition aligned two in the front and two in the back; or the proportions and all the characteristics of a car that appear for all the cars. We can imagine that if the car starts being very big, or with a trailer behind, in the beginning we may distinguish it as a car. If they tell us no, that is a truck, our car neuron will stop spiking when the size gets too big, and the size of a car will be then recorded as important.

In general, the descriptors that consistently spike when we see a car get reinforced. They connect stronger than the rest. This way the next time we see an object with these descriptors, our car neuron will spike.

Redundant information like the color, since it is not consistent, it is not stored as a distinguisher of a car. If color is reinforced in the beginning, it weakens over time, because the same color is not shown, hence it is not spiking all the time: it is not being reinforced, gets forgotten, and weakens.

The way it is storing that that object is a car is by the strong descriptors of a car. The neurons that are encoding these descriptors and spiked when appearing get connected to the car neuron. The connections of these descriptors get reinforced to give next time a higher electrical input. The rest of the descriptors, like any color, since sometimes may appear in the car concept but they may not spike and appear always, do get weakened. Eventually, only the descriptors of the car that spike consistently when somebody is teaching us that that is a car are the ones wired and codifying what a car is. At that moment dopamine levels do not deviate too much from its baseline secretion since now we do recognize cars correctly almost all the time.

When concepts are more stable and consistent then they get wired strongly and put in its optimal place in the brain while dreaming [37]. We can see then that sleeping is an important process for memory, learning, and change. It is necessary to sleep the necessary hours so that our behavioral change gets recorded more permanently, and our learning capacity gets rejuvenated in the morning. This is roughly how we end up learning to recognize a car–and any other thing for that matter.

The will to learn started the secretion of dopamine. The neurons involved in learning started rewiring when the task succeeded, remembering the situation of success. And this game of higher dopamine when a possible pleasure is perceived; lower dopamine to motivate learning to get it; and higher dopamine again to rewire neurons when the success happens stabilizing afterwards to normal levels, is the main cycle by which neurons wire and learn. They wire in different ways, and makes us more skillful, knowledgeable, or just more trained to do certain actions with success.

Some neurons transport ideas, others transform it

We will explore now the neuronal system with more detail so that we understand really how habits are electrically connected from beginning to end.

When we receive stimuli, these stimuli are activated electrically and send the signals to the next neurons. First, they receive activation from the senses. Somebody touches our skin; a photon enters our eye; or hairs of our ears are moved by the air sound waves. All these feelings are detected by our sensors, and these sensors create an electric impulse to the nearby neurons to communicate about it.

There are a lot of types of neurons. We could classify neurons in general by being sensory neurons, motor neurons, or interneurons. When we touch something, for instance, the little sensors under the skin react and send electrical signals to the nearby neurons. They in turn send signals to other neurons and, by a chain transmission, follow a path that goes directly to the brain. The brain will then know that we touched something, and if this something is smooth and such.

Sensory neurons are meant to get environment information. They usually activate in a burst of electrical spikes if the input is strong, and they adapt their frequency and quantity to the strength of the input. The higher the input, the more numerous and shorter in time are the electrical spikes. This means that we usually have the capacity to sense things up to a minimal point and to a maximum point, like heat. We get the strength of that feeling by how energetically the neurons are throwing electrical signals. Adapting the signal is important, for instance, to allow us to ignore background information like noise, or repetitive signals like would be a bad smell. Olfactory receptor neurons bind with a lot of molecules to send electrical signals with different patterns to convey the smell. Their spiking patterns are far richer than other sensory neurons.

Motor neurons move muscles and other parts of the body. They use the same mechanism of electrical bursts, but the other way around. When they burst with high frequency spikes, the muscles and other parts of the body move a lot, that is, move faster. When the train of spikes are more distant in time or with lower frequency, the muscles move slower. The brain tells the hand how fast to move, for instance, by the strength of the electrical signals that it sends.

The most common type of neurons are the interneurons. They are the neurons that transmit and process information. They only spike when the neuron receives enough electricity to spike, otherwise they keep silent. This mechanism is meant to transport information and codify it, like complex concepts. [38]

Once one neuron is activated, it is connected to other neurons in a way that one neuron can receive a few thousand connections from other neurons, and connect in turn to other few thousand neurons. There are billions of neurons in the human brain. And they create up to one thousand trillion synaptic connections [39]. For instance, certain neurons have been detected to codify a concept, so they may have a single neuron dedicated only to spike when we see or think about this concept, like would be the concept of the moon.

Something important to know is that a neuron, no matter how much electricity it receives, it will react with a spike always with the same strength: seventy millivolts. The information flows always in one direction. When a neuron receives enough electricity to spike on one side through its dendrites, it spikes at seventy millivolts and sends its signal to the other side of the neuron, the axon terminals.

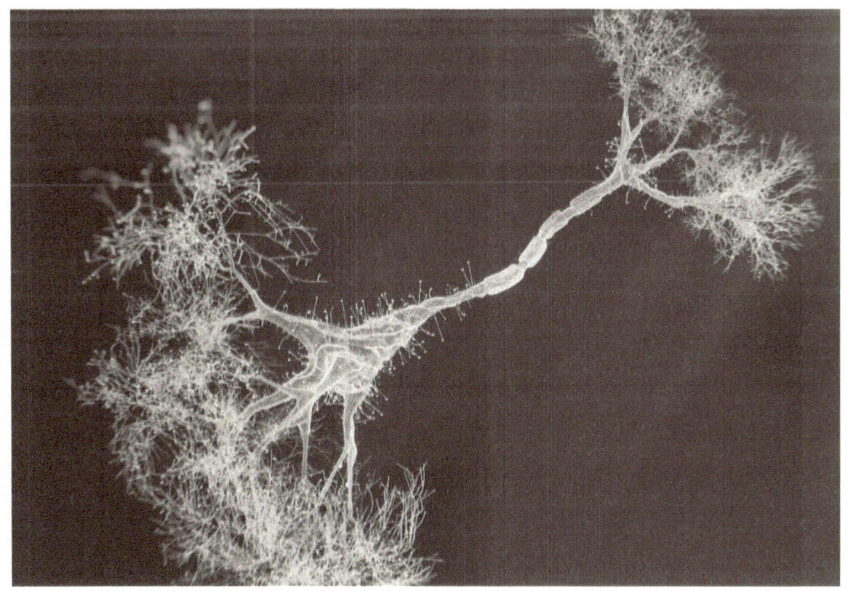

Neuron with dendrites and its core on the left, and axon terminals on the right

iStockphoto.com/koto_feja

When spiking, it gives electricity in turn to the neurons it connects to in a much lesser degree by using neurotransmitter molecules. These molecules generate a reaction that creates electricity on the receiving neuron through the synaptic connections between the axon terminals of the giving neuron, and the dendrites of the receiving neurons. This is for all neurons of our body, sensory neurons, motor neurons, and interneurons. The only difference is that, on occasions, instead of a single spike of seventy millivolts, they may give spike bursts of seventy millivolts once activated. At times the connections may also be inhibitory, which prevents a neuron from spiking, and it is very used to create memories [40] or to discriminate concepts.

In our moon case all the neurons that would have the moon descriptors would spike when we see the moon, making the moon neuron spike at seventy millivolts. The neuron in turn will send electricity in a much lesser quantity to all the neurons that are interested or related to the moon concept. If no other concept is connected to the moon concept, the signal will not activate other neurons.

Say though that we are watching a werewolf movie. Imagine that we see that the werewolf in the movie is now a human, and he is staring at a full moon. The concept of the movie, a werewolf, a moon, and in full form, will activate the neuron of a man transforming into a wolf. That is, the idea that the man in the movie is now going to transform into a wolf will start popping in our minds. That is because the neuron–concept–of a man transforming into a wolf is being triggered by other neurons, like the moon neuron, the full phase neuron, the movie neuron, and the werewolf neuron.

A neuron can be connected to thousands of other neurons, but each connection has a different independent strength flowing always, as we mentioned, from the giving end, the axon terminals, to the receiving end of the connected neurons, the dendrites. Once the neuron has spiked with seventy millivolts, the neuron activates in every connection of the giving end the process of transmitting electricity.

When a neuron spikes, it does not just distribute the seventy millivolts to the axon terminals till it depletes, what it does is to communicate to all the neurons that are connected to it that it spiked. It communicates that the concept or idea that that neuron holds is appearing somewhere in sight, in any sensory stimulus, or in thought; giving that information to all neurons that are interested or related to that concept.

Every connection must give electricity in whatever strength it is connected to another neuron. It may be different from one neuron to another. Every synaptic connection transmits electricity using neurotransmitters, so it does not really need the seventy millivolts. The seventy millivolts spike just activates the process of creating electrical signals to the other neurons. When a neuron spikes, it gives more or less electricity to other neurons depending on how strongly they are connected–how important is that concept for the other neurons.

The initial seventy millivolts are just saying to the neurons it connects to that the neuron spiked–meaning some sort of information activated it and is letting it know to the neurons that are interested.

In summary, a neuron spikes electrically at seventy millivolts when enough electricity has been received from other neurons, and this starts a process where every neuron that is interested in this knows about it. The neurons that are wired to receive information receive a certain amount of electricity independently of the seventy millivolts through the neurotransmitters located in the connection itself. Depending on how strong the connection is they will receive more neurotransmitters, hence, more electricity when the neuron spikes. This means that they are strongly wired if that information is interesting for the other neuron.

An example would be the fact of having seen a car. If other neurons are interested in that we saw a car, they are connected with the car concept by wiring themselves in the giving end of the car neuron. Once the car neuron spikes, they receive a certain amount of electricity to know about it. The stronger the connection, the more electricity they receive, and in turn it means that the more important for them is to know that we saw a car.

All neurons connected to a single neuron receive electricity almost instantaneously after the spike of seventy millivolts. What happens on the receiving end? As we mentioned, a neuron has a side meant exclusively to receive electricity from other neurons that spiked. That side holds a branch like structure called dendrites. The dendrites of a neuron receive connections from up to thousands of other neurons, each one connected by the synaptic connection. Every time it receives certain amount of electricity from a neuron in the way of neurotransmitters that electricity travels from the dendrites to the core of the neuron.

The core of the neuron, as we can imagine, is constantly receiving different amounts of electricity from the neurons that connect to it. The problem to make it spike, though, is that once the electricity is received, it wanes relatively fast, so a lot of neurons have to spike at the same time with an accumulated enough electricity to make the core of the neuron spike.

Imagine there is somebody, far away–a friend–and we want to call him. Imagine we are with a bunch of other friends and everybody tries to call him on his own timing and screaming. One says, "Daniel!" But Daniel does not hear about it. The other says screaming louder "Daniel!" And still inaudible. Everybody on his own timing starts screaming his name "Daniel, Daniel, Daniel…" And even if two coincide, Daniel is still not hearing clearly anybody meaningfully. Only when all of our friends agree to synchronize at the count of three. "One, Two, Three, Daniel!" Then is when the signal is strong enough to convey at once the information.

Neurons function in a similar way. If it receives information from other neurons at different times, the electricity wades by the time the next input comes. Only when they are received at mostly the same instant, they are summed up to have enough electricity to trigger a spike in that neuron.

Every neuron contributes with different strengths. A neuron may be giving eighty percent of the minimal necessary electricity to make the neuron spike, or five percent, or even so small as a hundredth of a percent–we would expect that with thousands of connections everybody would give just a little to the other neuron. It is though important to realize that timing is everything, and when spiking some neurons can be connected with double strength or triple strength compared with another.

Once we add all the connections that are going to the input, if enough input neurons spiked with enough force and close in time to each other, they activate that neuron they are connected to. The neuron that spikes in turn helps activating other neurons and creates a chain of activations. We can see, for instance, that to distinguish a car we have to see all the properties of the car at the same instant. It does not suffice to be shown now a wheel and now a chassis at different times to identify a car.

Usually the neurons in the muscles–the motor neurons– do not share much information. Only that the muscle needs to be pressed. If my brain wants to move my feet, it will send electric signals to my muscle, but it is not interested now in too many complications. It wants to move my feet at certain strength, so this type of connections is usually very straightforward. One neuron activates the next one and the next one until it reaches the muscular part. Then it activates an electrical charge to the muscle–it will shorten the muscle and create a movement. If somebody touches a hair of my hand, that feeling will be transmitted very directly from one nerve to the next until reaching the brain.

In the brain the complexity of the connections is manifested in order to process information that reached it, but outside the brain it is usually straightforward. The neurons of a type meant to transmit information efficiently are sort of bigger; covered with an insulator to maintain the electricity; and there are mechanisms for this signal to not get diminished while it is being transported through the long neuron's axon. It is like a cellphone signal tower would do. It would have like an amplifier at every point where the signal jumps back to its necessary strength–seventy millivolts–after every neuron spike to make sure that no electrical charge is lost, and that the same amount is transmitted until it reaches the brain.

This is in a nutshell how neurons transmit electricity: conveying some sort of concept or information. Some just transmit it, and others join different concepts to form an even richer concept. The magic is that only when we are perceiving that concept, thinking about it, or being part of another concept, the neurons of these concepts do spike electricity. The same would be for motor neurons. When they spike, they create movement. If we will to move our feet, the neurons connected to that intention start spiking, and in turn move the feet or any action we want to pursue.

Once attention is involved, the parallelism is limited, but in an automated mode we can image how these activities act in parallel and process a lot of visual, auditive, and other information at the same time. The greatness of the brain is that it does all of this in parallel; coordinating and processing lots of details of our daily life in an effective and convenient manner. It does it without us being aware, until we pay attention and choose to interfere, and change it for a result desired from our choice. When we do that, neurons not only change their patterns, but also choose to do those actions in the future more effectively, and in a more automatic way.

Neurons, and how they distinguish everything

There is a minimum threshold of necessary electric potential–close to minus seventy millivolts–that the neuron must reach to be activated. It always comes from the electricity received by the dendrites. When that threshold is reached by the core, the neuron is activated, and it spikes on the other end of the neuron, the axon terminals. Then it will be recognizing something.

Vision is very automatic, we see objects and we recognize objects, but we do not know how to recognize absolutely everything. For instance, I still do not know exactly what kind of trees are in my nearby forest–besides a few trees that are very common like a pine. I just do not know to distinguish trees. I just do not know how to distinguish mushrooms. I do not even know how to distinguish different fish in the ocean.

Why do I not know how to distinguish certain fish? Because maybe I did not need it, or I did not make the aware effort to learn it. I did not have to–it was not part of any plan. I never learned it, though I could, but never did, so I do not know them. Maybe I have seen these fish a lot of times, but I never stopped to pay attention–to learn it. Even though I was looking at those fishes I did not have sort of a reward pushing me to learn it, so my neuron was not aware. It never learned.

Let us say I do not have an activation neuron for, let us say, tuna. I do really because tuna is a quite common fish, but let us say I never wanted to learn how a tuna fish looks like. Maybe I do have a tuna neuron, but it is very vague and I cannot distinguish a tuna from a similar fish in taste like a swordfish. I have never made the effort–I have never paid attention. In the ocean it would be hard to miss a fish whose nose looks like a sword, yet again, if we spot a marlin, it would be extremely hard to distinguish it from a swordfish if we have never learned the differentiating features.

Attention is very important; the will is very important. This is how we learn: first we need to have a reward. There must be a reason why we are learning. Every learning is associated with an expected reward or pleasure for some reason–little or big–otherwise we do not learn. Neurons that have these little reward-seeking neurotransmitters activated–dopamine–just want to learn how to obtain the rewarding goal, so they are just saying to the neurons, "Let's learn", and they do learn. And the reinforcement of the connections start. We needed attentiveness to check if we are recognizing correctly, so learning also demands of our attention. And by being attentive we promote more dopamine signals to say, "Identify this correctly and I will know we are closer to the pleasurable reward in every identification."

When we want to learn behaviors, this is how it is set up. Our brain is full of connections, and it is full of neurons that are connected strongly or less strongly. The way it works is that every time that the neuron of a behavior spikes, the connections of the neurons that are connected at that very time, and contributed to the spike got reinforced.

Sometimes we have to learn basic concepts first to distinguish accurately higher concepts. We cannot learn higher concepts if we do not first learn more basic concepts that compose them first.

Using the example of the car, the strength of the neuronal connections representing the wheels of the car neuron are reinforced if we look at a car, because we see that it has four wheels. When the car neuron spikes, the wheel neurons that made it spike get connected strongly. If we see another car again with four wheels, the connection will get strengthen yet again.

The color factor may not get strengthened because it is possible that the first car was red, and later the second car was of another color—say blue. Mostly there will be too many colors to be determinant. The strength of the red color, for instance, is diminished if it did not contribute again to the car concept.

Let us say for the sake of accuracy that most of the cars that we see are very silver-like colored, so at least the neuron of silver-like color will often be activated. Some colors may not always be activated, but they will have some strength because a lot of times cars are gray, white, black, or with very shiny metal tones. These characteristics will be spiking with the car a lot of times, but not always, yet they will indirectly give us a hint that it is a car. The connections that are wired and do not contribute to the car concept get weakened, so finally only the main determinants of what a car is are the connections that will be left and reinforcing each time we see a car.

There is a normalization process where if one concept gets so strong that only by appearing the neuron spikes, and moreover it spikes for something that is not recognized correctly, all the descriptors get diminished proportionally so that the exploration of the properties that distinguish a concept renews, and the recognition becomes more accurate. This is necessary indeed so that there is a balance to explore all the properties that uniquelly identify something, and not one overwhelming the rest.

As soon as the threshold of electricity is reached, the neuron spikes, and one connection cannot be reinforced forever and contribute alone to that threshold, so the normalization process diminishes the signals proportionally in order to help the neuron hear other descriptors too. It forces the neuron to explore and distinguish all the descriptors of a concept, and not only using the first ones that hit the neuron–though nobody can deny how powerful first impressions are.

This is how it works. And it is very beautiful because the descriptors that always distinguish a car will get very strongly connected. Even the hints that may help us to distinguish a car get connected, maybe less, but they do help the neuron spike too. If it quakes like a duck, walks like a duck, and flies like a duck, it is very probable that it is a duck. Maybe they are not strong descriptors, but even the small qualities, if they get a little bit connected and they spike together, will have enough strength to conclude something.

We described neural visual recognition, but the brain uses the same mechanism for almost everything. The only point is that there are different neurons and different shapes. Some are narrow; some are distinctive neurons that spike at different strengths; others are neurons suited to the type of information complexity they must process. There are a lot of nuances with the neurons, but fundamentally the concept is this one: if they spike together, they activate the neuron together. A concept then is connected or related to the neurons that make it spike.

The brain uses mostly the same mechanism for a lot of things, including behaviors. Let us imagine for instance that it is six o'clock on a Sunday evening, and we are at home with no plan. What will our brain do? Our brain will process this information: home, six evening, alone. If we are not paying attention, this will automatically trigger a process–like a program.

Remember the descriptors of the car? Now we can see how other descriptors would be identifying an environmental circumstance, like a Sunday evening with no plan. That situation or moment, once identified, would recall an activity that we did. That is, when the brain recognizes that circumstance happening, it activates the activity associated with that circumstance, and the activity starts popping up on our minds. If we do not stop consciously for some other reason, it automatically moves us to do that which is programed to do. Once the brain starts this process–the neurons start spiking to activate this process–they start a chain reaction and start a whole bunch of neurons, so that we do the associated activity automatically. A simple neuron can start a whole bunch of processes composed of other neurons.

Let us say that we are at home at a certain time, and we already were before–the prior weekend–at home, at this time, in these circumstances, and we did watch a movie. Imagine we watched a movie a couple of times in this set up. This wired the circumstances with this activity strongly, since we repeated it a couple of times or more already.

Our brain will realize a few things. It will say, "All right, you are at the same time, at the same place, and in similar circumstances." It must not be totally equal, only matching enough to know that a movie was enjoyable, and that that is what we did before in these circumstances. So, it will suggest, "Why don't you do this activity again right now?"

The neuron will activate that process, and we will say, "Aha, let's watch a movie"–because we have done it before. We have wired that part. In case we do not think too much about it, or that we are not much aware, this is what we will automatically do. We will look at the television, we will see they are showing a good movie, and we will watch it if that is what we are used to do in these circumstances: we are moving in a very automatic way.

We do not want to fight all the time against our automations. There is a limit in the amount of awareness we can have. It will be tiresome if we try to be aware of everything and try to change absolutely everything to something different than what we are used to in a very short time. Indeed, automatisms are meant to save us energy, but when we can, we should be aware and change them to our desired actions if they are different from what we are used to do.

The reality is that if we have goals, we have to start achieving them. To achieve them we have to know what we want; what we have to be doing at certain times; at certain hours; and in certain environments. We already must know what we should be doing, and what we should not be doing. It does not suffice to say, "Oh, the plan was broken, it was not as perfect as I expected, something went wrong, so I will break it." This is not how it works. It is better to create for those situations an environment where we can do it. Of course, if we can do it with a full plan, let us go ahead, but if we are stuck with it and we cannot do it, there is an alternative we explored before: changing the habits–within a generic plan, and detailing the short-term goals.

Crafting habits: desire, awareness, and action

When neurons spike together, they create a remembrance. Every action that we do is recorded in our brain. Every single thing that we do since we wake up until we go to sleep is stored in a process somewhere. Even if we do not give significance to a small action, nor we are aware of it, in reality every action that we do is storing a connection somewhere. It is creating a connection of actions with some circumstance. It is remembering that action as a desirable action to be repeated again, unless it hurt of course. If it was hurtful or the body rejected it, it will not be wired as a thing to do, but as a thing to avoid, yet it will be wired nevertheless.

We have needs for our body, and our body wants comfort. Every time we break a connection that we have created before it creates a new connection, and this is tiresome for our body. It is consuming energy–more energy than usual–because we are rewiring our brain again; it is consuming more dopamine. Our brain will complain, overall if our physical predisposition or current energy or fitness is not helping. It will complain if the circumstances do not help our brain, until at a certain point we may feel it is too much.

The body is made of a lot of processes, and every single process we do every day is recorded. Have you ever wondered why if there is a dining room full of chairs we always sit in the same place? For the first entrance we had all the chairs in the dining room ready for us. There is no special reason we should choose one seat over another, but we do choose based on whatever criteria we thoughtfully considered consciously or unconsciously. After that we seat in the same place if there is no special reason to sit somewhere else. We will sit in the same place that we sat yesterday and the day before, unless a higher compelling reason moves us to change. But why?

It is like this because our brain stored that information already. We have sat in that place before. That connection was already established, and our brain is just triggering that connection—and it gives us a little bit of uneasiness if we do not do it. It is warning us that if we sit somewhere else without a more pleasurable or necessary reason, it will be a little more uncomfortable for it to rewire, so it prompts us to sit in the same place so as to not rewire that connection. And if we are not conscious nor change it for some other reason from our will, we will sit in the same place.

Every action that we do is stored in our brain, and it is stored as an action to be repeated: it is stored as a habit. And this is where we want to kick in the changes. We want to create habits, but we want to create good habits. And what we want is to create habits that are according to our goals, and lead us to our goals. Unbeknownst to us we will be doing these habits easily and good.

Once habits are practiced, they will be very automatic for us, because they will be already stored. And yes, we will think, "Why didn't I practice the good habits, and why did I do bad habits before? What is the reason? Why did I not started with good habits to begin with?" The reason is we did not have any reason. Our plans may had been broken right away, so we stopped creating them. We may lacked wisdom and understanding of the real consequences. We may did not know the pleasures that come out of good habits; or worst yet, that we missed by doing bad habits while we were looking for pleasures where there were none. We may not were aware of the real capacity we have to achieve great goals.

When we want a big reward, then is when awareness comes in. If we stop and start thinking, sit and visualize the goals we want with the beautiful and rewarding situation we will achieve as persons in our lives, and visualize its details, we create an expectancy of reward. If we truly visualize it, we prepare the rewarding moment we will be in, and we gain its associated will to do it–even though we have not yet been rewarded. Indeed it is known that the expectancy of reward is stronger than the reward itself to move us to do things.

Planning is good, but once a plan is broken we argue with ourselves why not doing something else. A plan may be the path to success, and it may brake. So, we may stop visualizing and start thinking there is no more reward–that is simply not true. Every action that we do–positive or negative–is creating a pattern for future moments. This action that may be so difficult to take now, just because we are not used to, or because it is the first time we do it, will be rewired as an action less tiresome to do in the future.

In the example of the chair, our brain will record it, and it will be easier for our brain to choose a place to sit the next time around. Even when the decision is difficult, we do it again, but with less effort. Another repetition still and it will be recorded again in our brain. The connection will be stronger, and even less difficult the next time. When we talk about choosing a chair it seems easy, but moving this to household chores, quitting a bad habit, or every time that we decide to do the right thing, we really rewire our brain to help us the next time. First comes understanding of what we want and where real pleasure is, and then training the brain by repeating the good actions.

The beauty of wisdom and of being aware is that if we keep changing smaller actions all the time, we can keep doing those actions with less effort. And that will lead us to where we want to be as persons in a very surely fashion. We can move to where we want in our life and in our goals almost effortlessly. If we keep repeating them and repeating them they get reinforced. In the beginning they may be very chaotic, and it may make no logic as to even say, "I don't see how these actions as a whole will lead me to this goal. These actions are isolated, and they have to be done all in the same day! How can I do that? It cannot be. I am not achieving anything!"

It is really like the car neurons. We see two wheels and we do not distinguish a car, just two wheels. We distinguish the wheels rather well though. Four wheels do not activate the car neuron either. There is a metal chassis on top, a windshield, and suddenly there is a point in which the spike of the car neuron gets triggered. And it will be triggered again and again.

Little actions that seem to have no effect at all and are isolated seem of no worth for our goals, but if identified as necessary, we must do them, keep them around, and repeat them. Eventually all the unconnected actions will join together in an efficient manner. They will start moving us to where we want to be.

Bad actions sadly are also stored. Every bad habit is also remembered when we do it even once. The strongest ones with higher dopamine—the addictive ones—must be identified and get rid of. They detract us from our goals. And they will be stored in our brain if we do them a little bit here and there.

This beautiful Sunday evening that we still have energy, and we could achieve so many things that sometimes we may say that we do not have time for, we may use it for an empty entertainment, for instance, or we may choose to practice a habit that moves us closer to our desired goals; we may choose to do something wasteful for no useful reason, or to profit the time to learn and do joyfully what we need and wanted to do all along; to waste some energy maybe, or to do an activity that recharges our body, heart, connection, and soul; to fall for something that never gives pleasure, or to embrace the opportunities to do the right actions that lead us to higher level pleasures or deeper soul goals.

Whatever we choose, that connection will be stronger next Sunday, and it will be more difficult not to do it, and easier to be done: we would have created a habit—and it is better to choose the right habits, and never or scarcelly what we know is wrong. We can create good habits and bad habits, so the way to proceed is to keep being aware of every moment so that we reinforce the good habits, and we get rid of the bad habits when they knock at the door. Every action that we do will be stored in a connection as good or bad; as useful or wasteful; as helpful or harmful. The frequency matters, and it is difficult to get rid of them if we let them grow.

Now we do have a plan, and we do have goals; we know what general steps to follow to grant us these goals; we know what single actions every day will lead us to those goals; we know what single action every week takes us closer to where we want to go. We know that, more or less, if we keep doing these actions, we will be in the path to reach our destination; that we will keep that direction; and that if we do it persistently, we will achieve what we are living for.

While acting is where our neurons get wired. While repeating is where our behavior is automated. By avoiding bad habits and doing good ones is where our energy and environment is more conducive to growth. All this is good, but still, Are we sure where to start? In what order? What priorities? How to deal with the hardships of growth?

This is what the next chapters will deal with: we will make strategies; we will understand our surroundings; we will understand our limitations; we will persevere; and make an action plan that will lead us to nowhere, but to achieve our goals. Follow me throughly with more details; to walk always with confidence; to be always our best selves; and to enjoy all this process with all our loved ones, and also in a way with the rest of the world.

Learn in order to do

Before we immerse ourselves with the intricacies of change, the daily struggles, and the road of growth, there is wisdom that needs to be acquired. Wisdom is more desirable than gold, and any endeavor that we do–from business, to personal, or life itself–needs its nuggets of wisdom that will lead us forward and pave the road we will always walk. Learning is key, and having some guidance of what works, what helps, and what we may encounter is paramount so that our lives enrich themselves with visions and expectations that are as close as what we will find. Let us not be afraid and embrace this new challenge of growth for life.

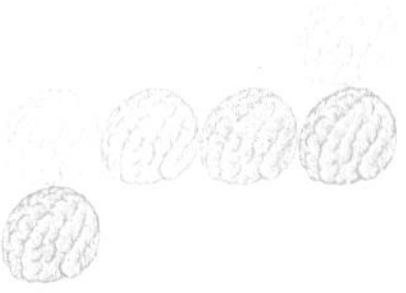

9

The road of the self

He used to say: If I am not for myself, who will be for me? And if I am for myself, what am I? And if not now, when? – Ethics of the fathers 1, 14

Most importantly, to know what we are living for

The path to growth is a personal path. Everybody has his/her own story. Everybody has his/her own travails. In the end we all share commonalities. Being lost is one of them–and it is one of the worst it can happen.

When I was eighteen years old a series of miss behaviors and uncertainties led me to a path I never thought I would traverse. All the plans that I had made since I was a child were blurred. I sacrificed a lot of moments for a goal; and the goal vanished, unannounced, and unexpected–at least by me.

When we are young we are still learning, but sadly we are carried away by a lot of conventions, ideas, paths, and dreams that are not our own; expectations and ideals that are not of our making–and this, sooner or later, takes its toll.

In the morning of Wednesday, April the eleventh of 2001, in the midst of the Jewish holiday week of Passover, and the Catholic festivity of Holy Week, I decided to go swimming to do a little exercise like I had been doing for the past years, and following my normal laps and training routines.

The previous day I had been playing soccer with some friends, and for some reason it left me stiff like never before –nor I have felt something like it since then. It encompassed my entire body: from head to toe. I could not even walk almost of the pain my body endured. That day, though, I decided to go swimming anyway.

When I was dressed in swimwear and went into the water, I realized suddenly that the pain had disappeared. Maybe it was because in the water my muscles were somehow unstressed. I started swimming. The swim was also good, and I felt no pain–even some sort of relaxation after having been all day with aches and pain in my whole body. I was comfortable in the water.

It was a sunny morning. I usually went late at night, since I used to go after school; but that day I went in the morning, and it was shiny. The day was nice. We had days off because of national holidays, and I just went to do my regular laps. It was not a normal day in a lot of ways, but I had not spotted the signs: the aching, the pain, and myself.

It was not a normal year. I had failed at school while I had always been an exemplar student. Somehow, I had never missed a subject for the summer, and I passed them all always with high grades, but the previous year I slacked– and I failed. I was lost like never had been before. It is not only that I missed some subjects, but I also failed the entire course. I always had some self-assurance that I would be doing good in studies, and I saw myself a successful student with a future career, but something was lost in the way, and I did not even know it.

The year before I got disenchanted with the studies. Somehow, I did not had motivation. I did not know what to study, and nothing was precisely my passion. But the problem was not that I did not have a passion–it was that I did not look for it. I just went with the flow doing the expected. Inside I was empty. I did not know who I really was, nor even asked myself what I wanted in life. I did it only once, and it was already lost in a drawer, along my many notes.

I was lost with the distractions of being young, with absurdities that lead to nowhere; and I never sat down to ask myself important questions. I thought the system had a path for us all, but it was not true. I was left on my own, on my choice, and on myself–and nobody prepared me for it.

So, there I was, repeating the school year while my friends were enjoying the first year of university–an awkward irony of destiny–a so dreamed goal for so long that I was still paralyzed, unmoved, and with shock while missing it. I was in an internal shock that nobody saw but me; in a slow pain that I only felt on my own; and it was not only physical. Such was the internal pain that I did not hesitate to go into the water to make some laps, even though my body was aching in pain from the day before.

Mentally I was in a state of not caring even about myself. I was numbed physically and mentally.

I started swimming, and it felt good. I was comfortable, and the sun was hitting me from the big swimming pool windows, reduced enough to enjoy my morning laps. Usually I swam in a hurry; but since I had days off, I just swam slowly, unhurried. I did not feel tired. I swam and I swam; and the clock said one hour, two hours. I noticed that it was already toping my times, so I decided to stop.

I had watched recently a movie where the actors took a few breaths before going underwater, and I thought:

"Wow, how cool it is! If I fill my lungs like this, What must it be like?"

This is usually practiced in free-diving, and I had seen it before big immersions, so I tried it out. I took some rapid breaths, and decided to swim underwater the entire twenty-five meters swimming pool. After swimming the entire pool underwater I realized that I still felt I had plenty of air to go back. So, there I was, extending my underwater swim another twenty-five yards without taking extra air.

Unsurprisingly I did not make it. After the second lap I was left underwater for more than five minutes, with convulsions–probably one could say dead–and with my heart stopped. Do not think I noticed anything. In my mind –or somehow as I remember–I was swimming in the pool. I remember I was swimming, but I was going unusually fast, almost as if I were flying on the water. I was underwater, but in my mind–or at least in my memory–I kept swimming and swimming on the water going very fast from one side to the other, certainly like a usual weird dream would feel like.

At that moment I opened my eyes. I was outside the swimming pool, and somehow a lot of people around me were paying me a lot of attention. I had been woken up, and suddenly a woman started asking me what day that day was. And I answered:

"Well, I think it is Wednesday if I am not mistaken, but I may be wrong."

Somehow, I felt that they cared that I said it correctly.

"Aha, he remembers! You had lost your memory for fifteen minutes." they exclaimed all of a sudden.

"Well, I do feel okay, so I think I can go now." I answered.

And they looked to me startled. I felt no pain. I felt good, and I did not understand yet what was going on. As the situation sank in I realized the pool was empty, and I was surrounded by very worried people.

Something big had happened there, enough to have emptied the pool of all the swimmers, and big enough so that I was being there looked at as the center of attention. When it hit me, all feelings came into place like a torrent of sorts. The first thought that flashed through my mind and really concerned me then was not of me dying, it was of the insurmountable loss I would have caused my parents had I ceased to exist from this world at that by very moment. Upon this realization I started pouring tears down my face.

How stupid I had been! When we hurt ourselves we do not only hurt just us, we affect other lives too, and that is why if we think a little about the consequences, sometimes we realize how stupid some decisions we make are.

The people around me told me they would call my parents to let them know. I replied that I felt okay and that I could go home.

"No, now you go directly to the intensive care unit. Your lungs are still with a lot of water!" they responded.

I was given an oxygen mask, and taken to the emergency intensive care unit of a main city hospital to ward off any potential damage I may still sustain. Destiny had me twenty years later programming hospital health equipment which that same hospital uses actively to monitor patients' health to this day.

Before, the doctor present at the sports center had just saved my life. I had been drowned for more than five minutes. And when rescued by the lifesaving guard, the resuscitation was then performed by the only doctor the center had and happening to come only on Wednesdays' mornings. She performed the full cardiopulmonary resuscitation.

Once taken to the hospital, I was placed in the intensive care unit room. Every doctor that saw my profile knew that the most probable thing that would have happened is to not have come back alive and healthy, but to have stayed there–dead. Every doctor repeated the same after reading the report: "You have been reborn."

I thought all was over, but it turned out I had to wait a few days until my lungs extracted all the water on themselves–which they did, blessed be G-d. I was sent to mental scans, hearing, breathing, and tests of all kinds to make sure no permanent or partial damage was endured, and all came out a total success, thanks to G-d–literally. I endured no damage at all.

Somehow after that day all felt different. I knew in a way all was the same–but I was not the same. It took me some days, though, to materialize and humble myself definitely, liberating myself from the shackles I had been enduring during those years.

After a few weeks I was approached by a teacher telling me that I was being disgustingly stupid after all that had happened. The problem was not external–the problem was on myself. I was being just as stupid as a person can be. And at that moment, unbeknownst to her, I humbled myself like I had not humbled in a very long time.

She was a teacher known to be weird, with talismans hanging over her neck, and a sense of rebellion and self-righteousness at the same time, with an allure of the sixties still living to those days. She was known to be able to make people cry with just a few intense words. Some people have talents–and that was hers.

I had never talked with that teacher personally before, and the only interaction had been answering correctly a supposedly rhetorical question about the name of the mathematician who proved that all mathematical theorems are fundamentally incomplete. I guess she was trying to lure her students to a more literary academic path, hinting us that mathematics were flawed at its core. Reality is that more than flawed they are not complete tools to describe reality.

"Gödel, his name is Kurt Gödel." I answered in a loud voice from the back rows of the class.

Thirty and so students woke up suddenly to the interaction waiting to see eagerly where all this was leading at. I think I expanded the answer, but I do not remember clearly now. Certainly I knew that his proof was based on the fact that all theorems have premises at its core–the accepted truths that start the logical deductions–and these premises are themselves assumptions that lack mathematical proof themselves, proving that mathematics are incomplete at its core. This proves hence that one cannot describe all existence with mathematics alone, and that mathematics are not fundamental truths on themselves, but necessitates that one accepts as true something unproven to start the logical deduction.

Gödel was one of the greatest mathematicians of the 20th century, meriting Einstein saying loudly that Princeton was his choice in order to enjoy having the privilege of walking with Gödel. I guess the teacher also failed conspicuously to inform us that indeed Gödel was also known for having proved mathematically the existence of G-d, and that moreover It must be unique and only positive. Gödel used high order logical proofs that are still being ratified with advanced computers and modern artificial intelligence to this day. Certainly a very important piece of information that was left out from our educational curricula. Let us not forget that he used mathematics to show that inside the mathematical system you need to add G-d to make it consistent, yet mathematics are still incomplete to describe fundamental truths themselves.

I did not interact more with that teacher until I encountered her later entering class weeks after I got out of the hospital—when she told me I had been disgustingly stupid. She knew my situation, and taking pity was not her style. Her style was a blunt direct truth—a piercing truth—that goes to your heart, and wakes up all the sleeping realties that one has been so afraid to see. After exchanging just a few words with her I was just brought back to life.

And while previously it was physical, now it was spiritual and mental too.

So, there I was, just two months away from maybe failing again in my studies, yet this time I had humbled myself. I just did the right thing: no crazy feats and not showings off. I just did the diligent work and expected its results. The results were not only As in pre-entry math exams, but I also carried them over in university till other distractions also needed some humbling all over again.

This story is not to show the feat of surviving a drowning, nor timed answers which I had just learned fortuitously weeks before. The story is to show that the world is bigger, and we sometimes do not see the bigger picture. As young, it is a classic that we get engulfed with the vanities of life, and make a buzz out of ignorance. We make something the whole world, and if this something disappears, the world goes with it–and this is hardly the case.

Life has a mission for us, and this mission is not always in the shape and form that we envision. Sometimes we find ourselves with strength and resources; situations and possessions that we assume are because we deserve them. It has nothing to do with deserving: it has to do with the tools needed to perform our tasks.

When we transcend the me and look for others, we start to see, we lose our blindness, and we get to see where we do fit in this big canvas called life.

The first step for growing is understanding who we are.

This means we need to know what our strengths are, and what our weaknesses are; to know what we enjoy in life, and what we disgust; what activities fills us with joy, and which ones we find better suited to do. Also it is good to know which activities are not really our forte. Getting to know ourselves is a task of exploration, of testing, of recollection, and of analysis. It may be clear to us, but we may need to explore things we do not know about ourselves. Having capacity to do things may not mean we enjoy doing them. Usually where we enjoy being at is really where we are meant to be; because life is a concert, and we do have a role. All is interconnected, and our contribution matters. It matters because it is our role—and we must enjoy it at its fullest.

We live in constant competition, with wealth as its maximum symbol of success, but this is independent. We may have it or we may not, but life is about doing what we feel and know we are meant to do: what fills us and what gives us purpose. What one wants in life may not be what another wants. We have to know what we are living for. We need to know what really makes us tick; what we enjoy doing. We must know what that thing is that we want to do, because while we do not know it yet, we may keep veering and looking just wasting time as if nothing matters—but it does. It matters because without us the world is a little empty. And we must fulfill our part to make it grow and glow in its intended purpose.

Knowing what we are living for is not only knowing what we want to do now. Life has many turns and twists, and sometimes we change our goals, or we feel like doing something else, but that is because life has different missions sometimes. We must reassess what we live for from time to time and know its ramifications. Maybe it is not only one thing, but different things. Let us identify them, and if we feel this is it, maybe we will never need to reassess it again. This is what we will aim for, and we will get there.

We must stick to the goals we set, and make plans for how we would get where we want. Goals and milestones will lead us to that destination. Where do we envision ourselves in a year, two years, five years, or the rest of our life? It is good to write down these goals. We must write milestones of where we should be at some points, and some plans in generic form on how to reach there. Not so detailed that we still do not know in what form we will fulfill them. We must dream big. Limiting ourselves–if it is not something obvious–is not good if we still are not aware of our potential or the opportunities we may have. We must aim big, something that would justify all the effort we do. We need something, or some situation we would really love to be in: a place with no limitations on how we would get there. Simply that it is the place we just want to be in.

We must know what to do to reach our goals, or what needs to be done to work for what we are living for. Sometimes lateral work needs to be done to achieve something else, or sometimes the path is more straight forward, but we need to trace a plan; a plan on how we would get to where we want to be, and follow it. We must make it more generic the further away we aim at; and be ready to readjust and reassess from time to time if we are moving where we wanted or we need to change something. We need to replan again sometimes, but not to be obsessed with planning. We just need to have a roadmap–to know where we have to go, and the path we need to traverse.

Assessing the day and energy giving habits: crucial

We must understand that in order to do what we live for–to reach our goals–we must establish good habits that harness energy and lead us to those goals. We need to get rid of habits that drain our energy and do instead others that harness that energy totally to be always in our full potential. We must make a list of the worst habits, and stop doing them. We also need to have good habits little by little by order of importance. We must prioritize them; keep habits that are necessary for living, that give us energy, that give us wisdom for our goals, or even some necessary training or activity.

It is necessary that every day we assess–before going to sleep or at quiet times–how our day went. Did we do what we wanted to do? Did we encounter something special that maybe we should have handled differently? Where could we improve? What are we missing? We must ponder about the day. Say it out loud to ourselves and make it real. We need to put it into words. We need to check daily how we progressed towards our goals. What we would do differently next time, what was missing, how it went, or what were its results. We should do it every day to keep being on track. Thinking about decisions with calmness, and committing to do things better next time is key to bring clarity and success.

We need to choose habits that gives us energy, like some exercise a week. Contrary to some beliefs, exercise also gives a physical and mental edge that helps us on our daily duties. It does not squander energy, simply puts the body in an active state, with an optimal heart pump, agility, and even mental focus [41]. Just by doing stretches and some little exercise we ignite the energy and the metabolism of the body to burn fat and get energy that lasts the whole day.

It is good to avoid clearly unhealthy processed foods with too many sugars, processed grains, or oils–foods that contain a lot of industrial ingredients with low quality. I would recommend eating varied food, but we are free to choose what to eat, and we also know how our body responds. I think though that universally, bad industrial ingredients add only poison to our bodies, which in turn must use energy to eliminate [42]. It is positive in general to eat food that gives us energy and health. It is also important to sleep early, rest, and wake up energized.

It is paramount that we do things with joy. We must care about the little details that make our day better, or our job and missions more fulfilling. It is key to avoid all bad habits that drain our energy and anything related. Only by harnessing the energy and habits that do positive things we will be in our full potential all the time.

Negative habits that lead to nowhere and really drain our energy in short and medium term are to be stopped immediately, even if after some training, but stopped as soon as now. We must be positive, happy, energized, and focused on our goals. We must realize that all negative habits slow us down, and only with full positive habits we act with our full potential all the time. There is a saying that when one is not going up, is going down, and we want to be always going up.

The choice is ours, and the distinction between real pleasures and counterfeit pleasures; or harness energy versus squandering; can only be made if we desire the real pleasures, our real potential, and our real goals.

We must choose what path we want to walk on, what habits and milestones we need to cross, and be always doing things that lead us to our goals. Physical or material true pleasures–or changing gears–are necessary here and there, but never losing sight of why this act is good, what benefit we take from it, and keep adding habits that only lead us to fulfill all we live for. We must use all the energy for those things that fulfill a purpose in our life.

We should take joy in all we have. While we do what we live for we always should be joyful with the resources we have to do it, with the things that enliven us, and focus on our missions and goals.

We must be serious in our endeavors and not joking around; avoid people that joke too much around serious matters, since it is usually or to undermine our pursue, or simply as an escape from reality. We must check our progress constantly, and just keep repeating the habits again and again while uprooting the bad habits, and never practicing them nor being associated with anything close to them anymore. By getting rid of the bad and doing good we will walk the path of our missions always with our full potential, with its full pleasures, and with utmost joy.

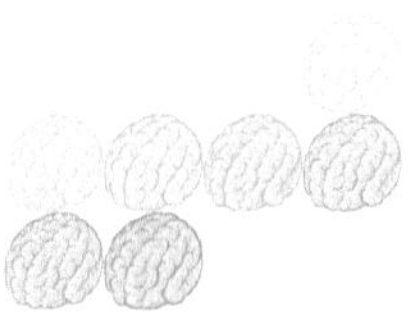

10

Do and do not look back

And it was as they took them out that one said: "Flee for your life! Do not look behind you nor stop anywhere in all the plain; flee to the mountain lest you be swept away"
(Genesis 19:17)

Repentance: the correction of our sins

Repentance is a process where we regret having done something wrong. Usually repentance is addressed to G-d, but the correction needs to be done to ourselves, or to other persons we have done something wrong.

The word repentance has other meanings too. In scriptures it is called return. Return means returning from a missed direction: we aimed wrong and missed the mark. We may not need to return from everything, but in certain things we may be aware that we need to aim more right.

The process of repentance is not difficult to do—but we need to follow its steps with care. Repentance involves doing just four steps: regretting, stopping, asking for forgiveness, and committing in our minds to not do the sin anymore. The beauty of repentance is that these steps can be done in an instant with all our hearts.

One of the most outstanding things of repentance is that we are cleansed of all sins and wrongs on the spot, though we may receive still some punishment if the sins were very strong. How can it be done so fast if there are habits that seem to stick around perniciously and lengthily untouched? That is because the first step involves a recognition that the wrong we want to correct is indeed wrong. The first step involves an awareness that the thing we did was indeed bad. But how can we stop that bad there forever if we have been used to do it for very long?

Being aware of our wrongs means that we explore all of its nature. To eradicate a wrong we need to delve into what we do think of it that we still attribute it as good. Usually, when we start analyzing, we may find that we have believed things that are untrue. We may have thought that when we do bad habits we get benefits and consequences that do not exist. We may have believed, for instance, that by doing bad habits we are looked at better, our body may appear better, or a lot of hidden attributes like pleasure or comfort may come along.

When we perform bad habits they never get the real pleasure we so desperately want. Bad habits distort the dopamine pathways in such a way that they create a seemingly endless illusion that, if we try another time harder, a lot of pleasures and benefits will come rushing in.

To be aware of the bad habits' illusion we have to be aware of how they started it all: a stress, a problem, a void in our youth, social inadequacy, or simply and plainly because we were utterly bored. Usually, when we start a bad habit others encourage us, or we have never been truly informed of its harm. A common reason to start bad habits is that others do it and it seems to not be a problem at all. The reality of bad habits is that not only they do not solve the problems we try to escape from, but they put them always on hold, and then in turn worst problems accumulate on top.

The good of it all is that we can stop them as easily as we started them all. All bad habits have in common that, besides the physical component of the dopamine and its neuronal links, they have perpetuated themselves because we have attributed to them–by associating thoughts–false benefits that they really do not hold. That is why any bad habit is first really started with an unassuming practice–be it because we felt anxious, stressed, we had a void in our life, or simply we felt utterly alone. Before that practice, if we recall deeply, probably we will find that we had really no compelling reason to do them at all.

To regret bad habits and finally stop them all we must analyze deeply the fallacies and fantasies we attribute to them that they very probably do not hold, or that we already had in spite of doing the bad habits. We have to understand that, if they are not right nor correct, all bad habits have zero benefits. They do not have nor the imagined pleasures that we see they boast, nor the comfort we attribute to them beyond the needed to calm down the stress and cravings that they create from the get-go.

Knowing that bad habits hold no pleasure is a deep truth that will help us always see past their ruse. By being aware of it, we will stop desiring them, and we will not get anymore fooled by their fraud. Knowing that they give no pleasure we will destroy them with the same ease as they tricked us all. We will destroy all its justifications and all the physical neuronal connections that they may still hold. After that, the only thing left will be doing felicitously what we always yearned to do all along.

Disentangling bad habits: all at once, and one by one

We all have heard about Sodom and Gomorrah. The family of Lot were accompanied by an angel in human form, and guided outside Sodom before the city was destroyed.

For those that do not know about it, Sodom and Gomorrah were really wicked places of ancient Mesopotamia that, besides sexual abuses, its inhabitants did things such as killing the older daughter of Lot by legal decree burning her alive for giving food to a needy person.

The family of Lot were advised to keep running and not to look back while the city was being utterly destroyed, but the wife of Lot, who still missed some of the wicked ways of the place, did look back. She looked as if missing some of that life–she died on the spot converted into a pillar of salt.

We must have clarity on what our priorities are, what we really want, and what attitudes are the correct ones. We must reach a point where we do not need to look back in need, but ascertain with full conviction that some paths are good, and others lead to destruction. We must have that in mind if we really want to succeed. Looking back is not an option, nor desirable too.

Not looking back does not mean we cannot analyze our past, it means not to look back to the bad ways in need for them. We must not entertain our minds with past wrong behaviors, nor attitudes that were clearly not positive: we must not look back to the old ways as if missing them, because that means we will be destroyed with them.

Once we have clarified the reality that they bring only destruction without pleasure, then we can abandon all physical linkage we have created with the bad habits once and for all. We need to identify what are the worst bad habits we have, and identify all its little habits and related behaviors which they hold. When we identify all habits as a one sole theme, we can assess better which little habits lead to the bigger habits, and how one behavior leads to another behavior to uproot them all. We need to know how little habits are related with stronger habits, and know absolutely how all the components are interrelated to be able to eliminate everything as a whole.

Before we want to eliminate a bad habit, as we explained previously, we need to know exactly why that habit is bad. We need to think about it, and ponder the fallacies we may hold that are not true. "I need this habit because such and such", "Without this habit life would be difficult to handle", or "I fear that by getting rid of this habit, I will suffer a lot." We must instead realize that we hold assumptions that are meant probably to keep us doing something that is totally wasteful, and the benefit of not doing the bad habit will probably prove the fears to be totally unfounded and false.

We should know from our hearts that the habit is bad, and that we are better off without it, and without its associated little habits. To do it we must understand that keep doing them is not only not pleasurable, but it will lead us to ruin in a lot of ways and we are really better off. We really do not want them, and life is more pleasurable without them. To test it, besides pondering why this is so and what wrong assumptions we have about any good we may attribute to these habits, we must simply just start stop doing them.

We must end up eliminating all the bad habits associated with a particular theme, little by little until all its neuronal connections and pathways are simply stopped from being activated, and weakened—or even erased. This way we will end up eliminating the bad habit and the little bad habits that lead to it. Most of the work is done when we are aware that they offer nothing at all: when we realize they hold nor any pleasure nor any benefit at all. Their physical neuronal connection may still be there, and we must know that clearly. Though it may take some time to eliminate, they do not pose as much threat deprived of the lies they fabricated before.

When we finally eliminate the bad habit, we are suddenly exposed to new energy, new experiences, and a new time that we may had never enjoyed. Our lives may get an influx of positive things that we did not experience so much before. We must be ready for it. We must start filling the void it creates with new positive habits that are aligned with our true purpose, and our true goals. We must stop doing the bad habits. and at the same time keep substituting them for good habits.

To do this I would recommend to stop all the bad habits connected with the worst bad habit we have for thirty days. A strong bad habit usually has a big connection in the brain; has a lot of smaller habits that are related to it; and moreover has associated a lot of bad assumptions that keep it there like "Others do it and it seems okay", "This happens to others and not to me", "It is not probable that this bad consequence hit me", or "I get lots of benefits from them all." Be it an escape to fill a void, just a small treat, or simply ingrained from us almost till we were young, we need to experience how life is without them and how much more we can accomplish taking back the resources it highjacks from us unaware from our part.

To start I recommend thirty days of complete avoidance of all the bad habits associated with our topmost bad habit.

From the story of the Nazir [43] that vows himself to be holy and to live a holy lifestyle, we learn that among other things he must spend thirty days as the default standard avoiding drinking wine, and being separated from all that reminds him of wine: like walking on vineyards, eating grapes, grape juice, or even the consumption of vinegar.

Then we find a law [44] that when Israelites are to engage in war, if a beautiful woman from another nation is held captive and one wants to marry her, he must shave her head, let her nails grow, and let her be in mourning for thirty days. After thirty days he has time to observe more things than only her beauty. The fact of being in mourning–which meant no relations–and having her hair shaved already helps taking the looks and physical factors out of the equation. It is understood that probably he may had abused of her while they were in war, and the circumstances were extreme and intense. After this period the heat of the moment–or the allure–is passed, and he can better assess if he really likes her or not, showing us that thirty days is a standard to quench addiction or attachment coming from a bad habit or an addictive behavior.

Anna Lembke, chief of the Stanford Addiction Medicine Dual Diagnosis Clinic at Stanford University and specialist in the opioid epidemic in the United States, shows in her bestseller book [45] how thirty days is what she considers enough time for the dopamine reward centers to go back to normal. She advises her patients to stop all the bad habits and related activities of any addiction–or considered strong bad habit–forever. Usually when experienced the benefits of stopping that bad habit, the deeper desire of her patients is to stay out of the bad habit forever.

Typical expected pain of stopping a strong bad habit and its related small ones is anxiety, irritability, insomnia, and dysphoria–that is, some feeling of unease or dissatisfaction. The good news is that if we wait long enough, our bodies reestablish our balanced levels of dopamine, and we can take pleasure in everyday simple rewards like would be going for a walk, watching the sun rise, or enjoying a meal with friends back again. With the realization of where real pleasure goes moreover we will be far and detached from the final innuendos of the bad habits death throes.

These in a nutshell are the working steps of stopping strong bad habits–and even addictions that we may have and have never recognized as such. Only by identifying those bad habits; understanding its nature and how they are really negative for us; wanting to stop them; and restoring the damage, we can start being aware and engaging in all the mechanisms to stop them. Only then we can stop them for thirty days, feel the difference, and accept any healing pain while filling its void with positive habits that are part of our purpose in life. At that moment we will perpetuate the change for all times to come.

Actions to disentangle bad habits			
Understanding the reality of its nature: if it is wrong, there is truly nothing good about it	Knowing that all the arguments that keep the bad habit in good view are lies	Identifying its related smaller bad habits or triggers, and habituating to avoid them	Not doing the bad habit nor all its associated smaller habits for thirty days
Distancing from people, environments, or situations that encourage the practice of the bad habit	Acknowledging waves of temptation as a reminder that bad habits use lies with no real pleasure at all	Better sleeping, healthier eating, higher exercise, and a calmer mind meditating or praying to G-d	Knowing what we want to do or achieve once all our energy and higher power is greatly restored

Knowing why we need the good energy and what we want to achieve with it is essential to have the drive to improve. The energy, spiritual bliss, and power that liberating ourselves from bad habits gives us must be harnessed and focused. What are our higher desires? Is there something that escaped from our grasp before? Do we want to use all this energy and spiritual bliss to achieve something we may not before?

When we are liberated from bad habits we get special abilities and powers. We get blessed with success in ways that we never had before. It is important that we always have in mind what we are living for, or in the short term what things we want to achieve or do better with all this new energy infused. Once we liberate and use all our potential, we will exceed our success in ways we did not imagine, and we must be ready to channel all this energy to the things we want. Knowing what we live for already paves the way with goals and achievements we expect to obtain.

Abandoning ourselves to the whims of destiny is not only bad but wrong. We must always keep our drive and will to succeed–it is our duty, and it is our job.

Entangling good habits for our own good

These thirty days are a suitable time frame to start doing and creating good habits, be it that we are eliminating a bad habit or not. Thirty days is a good time lapse to root habits that we want to include in our lives, habits for our wellbeing, and habits for the consecution of our goals; goals that are part of what we are living for.

We must get all the good habits that we want to do and locate them in a place during the week or during the day if daily. We must know beforehand when we want to do these habits, or in what circumstances we should be doing them. It is recommended to keep adding just a small part of the habit–minuscule where it should go–if we are not used to it. We must start small because otherwise we will be overwhelmed. We must start growing the habits that we consider priority, and keep repeating them and growing them over time until they fit organically into our schedule.

We should keep checking them and see if they are moving us towards where we want to go, or if we need to adjust some of the habits or schedule. We must always be positive that all will turn out okay, even though we may see that initially the habits are performed clumsy, small, or out of schedule. It may happen that we do not do them exactly as we planned, that perfection is not achieved, and that our path is not exactly as we envision, but we must know that at the end we will achieve our goals, even if in the beginning not everything seems to fit.

To achieve this is paramount that we examine daily how our day went. Examination in general is key in business and any serious project. For our life these are moments where the automations of the brain disappear, and we are really aware of all we did. In these calm moments we can program our minds to do things differently. We can decide to do certain things better, or stop doing things we realize we are better off not doing the following day or occasion it presents.

Keeping a day's review is a habit on itself that we need to develop. We need to write a diary, a report, or talk to ourselves. We must use any way of staying for some minutes assessing the day. We need to be planning ahead and analyzing our progress. We can make it enjoyable with a video blog, or simply talk to ourselves in the mirror, but we need an often assessment. It is better to do it daily to check how we managed during the day. The form does not matter as soon as it works for us and we say it into words, written or talked, but be it a habit or daily ritual that we hardly miss. This is essential in any business project, in any sports team, military operation, and certainly in our lives.

Once we know what our milestones are and what habits we should be doing during the day or the week we need to be in constant awareness. We need to ask ourselves often what the right thing to do is now. We need to examine our inner self to see if the action we are about to do is desirable or not, good or not, or right or not. We must intuit it from ourselves; from our purpose; and from itself. We need to be aware of what habits we are doing, and which we should be doing at every moment. We need to be aware and change immediately if we catch ourselves doing a habit we should not be doing, and do what we should instead. There are rules, and we must achieve everything the right way. Even if it takes longer, there is a right way and a wrong way of doing things, and the right way always succeeds.

Now the question arises, What is the right way? For all that we want to do there is a wisdom associated that we are better off knowing. We should make a habit in our lives to acquire wisdom in constant basis. We should dedicate a time during the day, preferable at the same moment or circumstances, to acquire wisdom and make it a habit. We need to know what the right thing to do is in our job, in our life, and in the projects we want to do.

The way to start is by always acquiring wisdom and knowledge. We must force ourselves to dedicate some time during the day to acquire pure wisdom for all that we need or in life in general. We must identify reliable sources we can trust, read, visualize, or listen to for some time during the day without a pause. We must never forget that wisdom is more desirable than gold.

Once we engage in this business of habit making and of walking our path, we can see that there are tools or resources to do our desirable tasks. These are our bodies and the environment. For ourselves energizing our body with some muscle stretching is the bare minimum to activate the organism, burn some fat, and generate energy. As one sees fit, some joyful exercise a few times a week may give us further endurance, agility, and physical and mental improvement too, overall if we do not move very much. Everything needs its middle term, but being angry–which zero or faking is the desirable trait. In everything else we must find the middle goldilocks amount.

Healthy energizing food is essential to activate cells in our body and be at our best. Extra vitamins are good too if we do not take too many fruits and vegetables. Vitamins are a good complement to make sure all our organism has the minimum nutrients. Vitamins can be taken naturally, of course, but that is if our diets are nutritious enough. Vitamins are the only nutrients that rarely the body can make itself from other nutrients, so they must be taken explicitly. Omega-3 capsules are a great complement too.

One day I was all day with my father when he got ill, and was later diagnosed to have the infamous COVID-19 pathogen. We had been all day both together without masks. He went to the hospital very ill the next days, so it seems it was already incubated, and we did not know that before. All I remember was a little throat ache, and my tests saying negative infection. I have taken vitamin complements for decades, and all exams have always showed good in most measurable levels of health.

I recently stopped taking extra vitamins because I emptied my last bottle, and the shop I used to buy did not have any left. I did not complement my meals with fruit nor vegetables strong enough either–something good not only for vitamins but also for fiber. Days later I was exposed in a work meeting to high cold winds, and as a result I got ill the very next day. After realizing I had not taken vitamins for a while I bought the bottle and resumed the habit of taking vitamins. After a few days I recovered from all. Now I take more fruits and vegetables because it is a better source.

The only time I did not checked good, even with vitamins, is when I abused processed meat food. Once I was eating with a very young twenties coworker that said he always ate meat in his meals. I already got the intuition that that must had been dangerous for his body if not stopped. I wish I had said something. He died months later of a heart attack without a warning. He had been looking good the days before. One Friday he was normal, the next Sunday he was gone. Not inferring this will happen to one at all because one eats meat daily. He had a heart condition before, but certainly meet is not good when processed and in excess–overall when we are talking about the heart [46].

Milk is not so good either when abused, and overall having passed certain age [47], but that is something each of us must explore and identify on our own. Usually the food where we live has naturally the best nutrients for that existent climate.

Mediterranean diet is flexible, really universal, and winner for several years in a row as the healthiest diet on earth [48], with olive oil as its nutrient insignia. The top contenders always agree on avoiding processed food and eating meat in moderation, favoring fish instead–but that is a personal choice. We must not to feel sluggish, but energetic and healthy. At the end of the day all food gives its nutrients, it is a matter of avoiding excesses. For that reason natural food is favored in place of added sugars or ultra-processed unhealthy oils, cereals, and meats [42].

Having joy in all that we do and a positive inner happy mindset coupled definitely with an early good sleep is the key combination to start the day with all the best we can give. Every time we go to sleep there are physical factors that affect us like, noise, heat, extreme cold, light, caffeine, excitant substances in our bodies, food close to our bedtime hours, or too little necessary nutrients too. Some substances that we may think help us going to sleep like alcohol may wake us up in the middle of the night without our proper sleep.

Caffeine too may affect us, since half of it still stays in the body after six hours, and blocks adenosine receptors from binding and creating sleep [36]. Based on some studies [49] we should consider any brain stimulant to be taken moderately no closer than four hours before going to bed; and eating our proper nutrients to let the body sleep correctly, which in case of emergency, a spoon of honey may do.

We must watch out for the physical factors to sleep properly, but obviously there is a psychological component too. Life is complicated at times, but we must focus always on ourselves. We must understand that there is a higher power that controls everything, and we must focus always on our progress. We must understand that what one day is of one color, the other day may be of a different one, but we must always focus on who we are instead of blaming others.

Usually it is a good technique to ask ourselves what is the right thing to do. Forgiving and asking forgiveness is an immense tool; judging positive too. Just focusing on oneself and letting events unfold once we decide to act correctly is the way to go. We must go to sleep knowing that we do not have grudge against anybody; judging positively as much as we can; and knowing that sometimes, if the events are not of our liking, the Ruler of the universe decided so, and we must just keep being good in our path.

Everything is for our own good, and more often than not we imagine illusions that are not real. In case of doubt forgiving, checking what we may correct in ourselves, and keep being righteous will just produce what must happen, and what is best for us. Meditation or prayer is of great help too.

It is important to realize that gossip is a very destructive practice. To speak gossip or to hear gossip is one of the most destructive ways of creating false fears, imagining things that are not, and complicating human relations. I would recommend staying out of gossip as much as possible. It is important that we always know our value, what we are good at, where we are not, and who we are. This way we will not be at the mercy of others' opinions, and we will trust in ourselves.

We must understand that ridiculing somebody in public—or even in private—is something very low and undesirable. We must never be dragged by haughty games, nor by the search for honor, because honor goes to the one who is less looking for it, or better yet, to the one who honors others. Anger in turn is a way to make our brains stop working and lose grasp and control of the situation; so the best is to never be angry; judge positively; and just do the right thing in every situation. We should assess the situation calmly and be mindful that we may be wrong or we may be right, but we must always do what is the proper thing to do.

Once we have our energy at full potential, proper sleep, physical activation, and nutrients, we must assess what are our environmental factors. We will work in an environment, and with external tools; that includes from our physical looks, to our physical environment, and also the physical tools we will use to do our goals.

We must not neglect the order and the cleanness we need in our environment. If it can also be beautiful and conducive to growth we should make it so. The cleanness and order outside are an extension of the cleanness and order inside. When we effect a change on our exterior, this immediately translates into our interior.

We must have a place where we enter and are good, energized, and ready to work; or serene, calm and able to relax, depending on the need.

This is one of the habits that for some seem menial, but it is of paramount importance. Cleanness and order is a reflection of how we are internally. Only when we have a tidy and clean environment, joyful, and we have habituated ourselves to keep it this way without much effort we will make use of fully energized surroundings with excitement everywhere we go.

Marie Kondo in her book [50] shows us how having a joyful environment with a proper order and keeping only the things that bring us joy helps us gain space and harmony every time we walk on that environment, and that that can effect profound changes in our lives.

The main guiding principles of Marie's method is to keep only the items that spark us joy; doing this we declutter our space, and later we can find a place for every item we own. The main ways she instructs us to achieve these goals is by first visualizing how we want our environment to look like. Once envisioned, we must tidy by category by putting all the items we own of that category in one spot; and keep choosing one by one if it sparks joy, if we love it, and if still has a place in our lives. If it does not we should discard it gently and thanking it for the use and service it gave us—be it that we learnt a lesson, be its decoration, or be it its usage in the past.

The main reason she recommends an ordered set of categories—be them clothes first, then books, papers, miscellaneous items, and lastly sentimental items and keepsakes—is that it is easier to identify if they give us joy in this order, since we learn easily on the first ones, and can keep perfecting this intuition as we move through. Any group of items big enough to fit into a category on its own—like bathroom, kitchen, or garage items from miscellaneous items—can be classified into a new subcategory and used to select elements of that category. This way we avoid too many items that may not fit in one spot.

Once we have kept only the things that spark us joy and donated, sold, or thrown away the rest with thankful feelings, and done it category by category; then we can start finding a place for each item, that is, its designated spot. Each item should have its own spot so that we can put it back in its place when not in use. Important to her is that all the items of all categories be first classified; and once the discarded are sold, thrown, or given away we can start finding a spot and storing them category by category.

For storage she recommends storing similar items together in order of thickness towards the thinnest, and by color shade towards the lightest. She also recommends folding almost every cloth that can be folded and that is not big or sensitive enough to require being hanged like coats or very fine cloth. She realized that by folding clothes, even socks or shirts, they never get wrinkled really, and by storing them vertically they are never being pressed by the top part like would happen in a stockpile.

Her main recommendation then is folding all the clothes in a square shape, to the height of the drawer it will be stored, and storing things always vertically, including papers or miscellaneous things too. In case of needing extra space we can reuse beautiful shoe boxes or other boxes we may already have, this way we can have items really visible and ready to be picked up, almost as if they were books on a shelf, only that horizontally too. She recommends doing it in an event like mode, not just small daily, because this is something that we want to do fast and just once in a lifetime, this way it can be done in a span of around six months for a common place. Once ordered we can just develop the habit of always putting things back to its designated spot when they are not in use, even contents of our bags.

We need to start somewhere, even if small–ridiculously small. Any action is better than no action, and perfection cannot come if we do not do it imperfectly first. Stephen

Guise shows us in his book [51] that when we start just doing a minuscule part of a habit, it is easier to do, it starts wiring the habit itself and allows it to grow later on.

Energetic habits			
Sleeping well the necessary hours	Moderate stretching and exercise	Mediterranean or healthy diets	Being clean and ordered
Doing things with goals in mind	Praying or meditating	Reviewing the day and priorities	Doing things with joy

If we continue knowing what we live for, having a plan, checking the progress daily, destroying bad habits, and repeating good ones, we will be at the height of our potential, and we will have all the power to do always what we really love.

Habits we can do for our own goals
iStock.com/limeart

11

Time to shine

Arise! Shine! for your light has arrived, and the glory of G-d shines upon you. (Isaiah 60:1)

Humbleness: the root that keeps us grounded

The first rule to start shining is to know that we are not in control of everything. As difficult as it may seem, humbleness is the first rule to keep up during all our endeavors. We discovered what we are living for, we set goals, and they can be big and great goals, but nothing stands in the side of haughtiness. When we are doing great the tests abound. Suddenly we feel good about ourselves, we are succeeding with our goals, and this is great, but there are certain rules that we must keep up.

Humility is the result of understanding a piece of reality, we are really given skills and traits from birth. During life we experience how certain resources are granted to us, and while performing a task, a lot of seemingly fortuitous circumstances creates and finally determines success.

We are not in total control, yet we do have free will, and we are expected to act as if we had control of everything–but reality is different. Even the success we may be experiencing after our hard work growing ourselves may be granted only so that we do something with it.

One of the ways to stay humble is to understand that, even though we may have worked hard for something, the truth is that we are assisted in a myriad of ways, and the resources we possess are also meant to be used. We are meant to enjoy them: wealth, wisdom, strength, and blessings in general. But we are also meant to use them for a greater good; as part of what we are living for; for the world at large.

If we do a daily accounting, moreover we check on ourselves often, and also talk to the higher Source–if we have it in our lives–it will be an effective way to keep us grounded in reality. We will be true to our purpose, and also correct deviations of our pride along the way.

One of the best ways to keep the blessings is sharing them: to share wisdom with somebody in need; to share wealth with the poor or needy; or to share strength to those afflicted. These are also one of the best ways to keep us rooted in reality, stay humble, and still enjoying our missions and the results it brings to the world, to others, and to ourselves.

Humbleness must be internalized mentally. Even though we really may possess virtues and are to be used, we also have faults, had faults in the past, and our success has usually come with a granting of factors that others may not have had to begin with. Our success is part of our mission too, and we must learn how to use it for good instead of being overwhelmed, squander it, or shine it off. We must not. We must embrace it, but with utter humbleness.

The first thing to do is acts of humbleness: give to persons in need; share wisdom; help people; shy away from honor; give honor to others; conduct ourselves in a respectful way and not a disdainful manner; and learn to accept that most of our success has been really granted, so we should not demand people to give us prizes. If we worked hard for it, it should be because it is our duty, not because we look for honor.

Certain personalities give more importance to honor than others, and this is a trait given for a reason, but that does not mean that our seek for honor has to run amok; simply that we must be careful to honor others, because it matters, and indeed even if we do not do it for the seek of honor we may receive honor in return.

Another act that helps being humble is to accept criticism. Even with evil intentioned insults we must react doing the right thing. This rarely means returning back the insult, but understanding that the Creator chooses to rebuke us through a person ready to do evil—or in a hidden source of love. The end result is that we will learn a lesson for previous wrong doings, and be cleansed spiritually; the evil executor will probably be punished if he does not revert his evil ways, and a good-hearted adviser will be granted reward if done with pure intentions.

We must understand that being humble means that the same that success is something ultimately given, protection is too, so by keeping being righteous we must not be afraid of fears in our heads about nonexistent consequences, but just do the right thing, stay humble, and heed the course.

If we are shining our soul that means we have surpassed a lot of impediments, and we are getting cruise speed, but that necessitates to assess daily how we are progressing. We must use special occasions to review what we live for, review our plans, make corrections if needed, and always keep our great work with constancy and trust.

Habits to manage success

Besides honor a successful situation also brings a myriad of distractions and things to deal with that we did not have before. We must follow examples given in previous chapters: to keep being righteous under duress; to stay firm to our convictions and values; and to correct and take the reins back if something veered us temporally from our course.

In the book of Stephen R. Covey [52] and his extensive research he recommends us to differentiate between something urgent and important, and giving priorities to some tasks over others. This helps us sort out the day. Having a clear mindset of which daily goals are priority helps us discard distractions that, though may seem urgent, are not important. He also discusses that we must keep learning which tasks to focus on, and accept that maybe some things must go out of schedule. We must keep knowing always, more or less, how much time we could dedicate to something, and which are the priority goals or items to achieve.

It is important to choose how to react to a given situation. It is paramount to deal with situations of conflict that makes us feel down. This is similar to the stories explained before where we may be in certain situations that are not planned, or that we did not expect, and we must train ourselves to react correctly, and to readjust plans and goals if needed. We must accept our wrong doings, correct them, and keep advancing. We control what emotions we associate to any event, so if we know something is not working our way, being down is not a response, but readjusting; accepting what we cannot change; focusing on what we can change and brings us joy; and keep advancing with righteousness knowing that at the end all will end up to our advantage.

It is necessary to check that we keep our energizing habits, and that in general all the habits that we built and unbuilt are also kept. We must always keep learning wisdom and keep adding good habits if needed. We must also keep uprooting other bad habits that we may still possess, so that we keep perfecting ourselves. We must perfect ourselves as if we were polishing a diamond. Our job is a constant work of perfection to be always the best we can be.

This improvement stage we are at may force us to deal with many overwhelming new situations that may come all of a sudden. We can use moments of solitude and serenity, like can be daily prayers or meditation to keep us connected to the higher Source, and tap it to get back a renewed state mentally, spiritually, and physically if needed.

If we do not have moments of solitude, we can go to inspiring places, locations, awe experiences, or sights that ignite our inner charging and connection.

We must establish daily goals we can accomplish, even if they are ridiculously easy to do in the beginning. We can start doing hard habits small first so that we can root them easier as habits, and by repeating them later grow them to its proper form.

The brain craves for reward, and craves for reward to wire the activity or the habit as something to be repeated. If our goals are noticeably big and lofty, we need to break them down into very achievable goals that we know we can do and we will do. Every reward matters, and the brain must understand that we committed to do a task, however small it is, and that we finished it. Once the task is accomplished, the brain needs to be rewarded by the feeling of joy from a task well done while seeing its results.

In the long run everything will turn out okay if we trust it will be so, because there is a system, a higher Power, G-d, Who makes it so—if we just trust in Him. The point is that in the meantime we need to do small achievable goals. Once completed them, the brain receives a reward in the form of dopamine for that feeling of achievement, and we want to finish our tasks so that dopamine is secreted, our neurons wire, and the next time that we do this task it is done much more easily.

Games know this concept very well. Prices are given early on with a lot of noise and bells dangling with exaggeration so that our brain understands that it got a reward. We need to do the same with our goals: create small achievable tasks, do them, complete them, and mark them as done; with beautification or fancy signals, noise, music, or anything we find appropriate to let ourselves know that we did a great job. We can make it fun like a game.

We need to understand that the core of success is to keep going. We must be positive in all the circumstances. In any setback we must humble ourselves and accept whatever happens, and keep working and fixing it while knowing that all will turn out okay. Everything that happens is so that we improve, our growth improves, and we keep going with utmost energy. Most successful people or businesses accept errors or mistakes and do not shy away from them; simply, they commit to correct them and to do it better next time.

We need to give things a proper time and priority. We should always prioritize things. What is the most important thing that we want to accomplish for the day? How much time have we allotted to each task? Letting work past its normal hours is dangerous because it eats up all the other essential habits we have for our goals. We need to respect the time allotted for things, and prioritize which ones must be necessarily done beyond others.

We need to check in constant basis if we have peace of mind, if our energy habits are in check, and if our most important habits are in place. We need to perfect all our habits and keep perfecting our duties and our progress, examining goals, and finding ways to do things always better.

When we do the right thing, we must have no fear; we must have no fear of opportunities, they will turn out okay; we must have no fear of change, it will turn out okay. The reason is because we are doing it because it is right–and we must never fear doing the right thing.

One of the things we must always keep doing is studying wisdom. When we grow there is always wisdom to be known about the tasks we do, about the problems we have, the opportunities, the life of others, and most importantly about life itself.

There are a few advises to study faster and good. Jim Kwik [53] in his book explains how clearing our minds and attaching a joyful feeling to learning make learning more successful; having a purpose and goals while learning keeps us engaged; stopping a little every twenty minutes and reviewing what we have learnt keep retention; and having a clean and appropriate environment keep us focused. We ought to be focused when studying and taking lessons while avoiding any distraction that may hamper our attention. We can review the learned material another day to retain it further on–and we must enjoy learning wisdom.

I remember I became proficient once in a university subject by reading the official book twice. The first time I remember I got muddling and weird concepts, but they started resounding in my brain. On the second pass all was connected and I internalized it like I had not done in a long time. The subject was Graphs and Complexity, so I took it very seriously to learn it as best as I could. Needless to say, I nailed the exam after that much effort, though I was not expecting it.

Most successful people are readers, and they read extremely fast. At times though I would recommend reading aloud to hear ourselves. We must choose what suits us best depending on the information or the situation, but reading fast is a good skill to have. We can train ourselves for it. We can do it just by counting how long we take to read a number of lines of a book, and reading the same number of lines of the following content to see if we improve our reading speed. After a while we will be proficient at reading and understanding fast. We will be reading, learning, and having joy like never before.

Attitude of growth

The blocks we put in our lives are blocks that do not exist most of the time. We can see, for instance, people with initial unideal conditions achieving great feats, or poor people becoming rich. Whatever assumptions we have that we cannot do something, or that we do not have enough capacity must be proven false by pushing us hard to see if it is true. If we yearn very deeply to do a thing, chances are we will succeed.

We all have a mission. All elements in nature are endowed exactly with the faculties to do what they are meant to do. If we explore deeply who we are, what we enjoy, and what we are able to do; we will discover that we are meant to do what we always dreamed, and what we always yearned. Usually we have abilities to do them. With effort and trust it will become a reality. The world needs our skills, the world needs every single one of us, and we must wake up and fulfill our purpose. With determination and patience we will be who we are meant to be, and when we do it nobody will take that from us. Once we know who we are we are there to finish the job. We must be patient and be who we are meant to be.

Before we saw in Proverbs that the righteous falls seven times and wakes up before succeeding. Seven is a number often seen in the world. Six is for nature and the seventh for perfection: seven days a week, seven planets, seven oceans, seven lands, seven organs, seven cavities in the face. When we have tried it all, when we thought we could do nothing else, then is when the moment comes: the eighth attempt, symbolizing an element beyond this world –a miracle of sorts.

When we have given it all, let us be prepared, because we will shine like never shined before; we will rise like never rose before; and we will be as joyful as we have ever been before, because then all will make sense. Everything that happened before will have led us to that moment: to the moment of completing our job.

Person completing his job
iStock.com/Chonlatee Sangsawang

We must never stop; we must never quit. We will succeed because this our destiny. Simply we need to give it all at all moments.

There is only one thing that is between where we are now and where we have to reach, and this is ourselves. The full humbleness and desire will break the most unimaginable odds we can fathom. That is why we are here; that is why we have these drives and these travails: so that we grow ourselves as far as we can reach.

Asking the right questions

In order to avoid pitfalls that we may encounter we must use the habit of asking ourselves what we would do in certain situations. It is a good habit to question things. It is good not only questioning what we are living for, but why we do what we do. Why do we choose one thing over another?

Asking the right questions is always the best way to understand the deeper meaning of things, the motives, and even to spot inconsistencies. It is good to learn, examine, and analyze the things we encounter with detail. It is also good to dissect them so that we learn their true nature. We must ask deep questions and not take things for granted. We must not be afraid to ask questions. We must ask others, and most importantly ask ourselves.

Analyzing issues is a good exercise to get clarity on the path to pursue, on the reality of things, and on the best options to muster. It is a good thing not to accept all we are told without first exploring ourselves the reason or analyzing first its veracity. This way we will not be blindfolded nor fall into traps of deceit. Sometimes a simple logic can spot many inconsistencies.

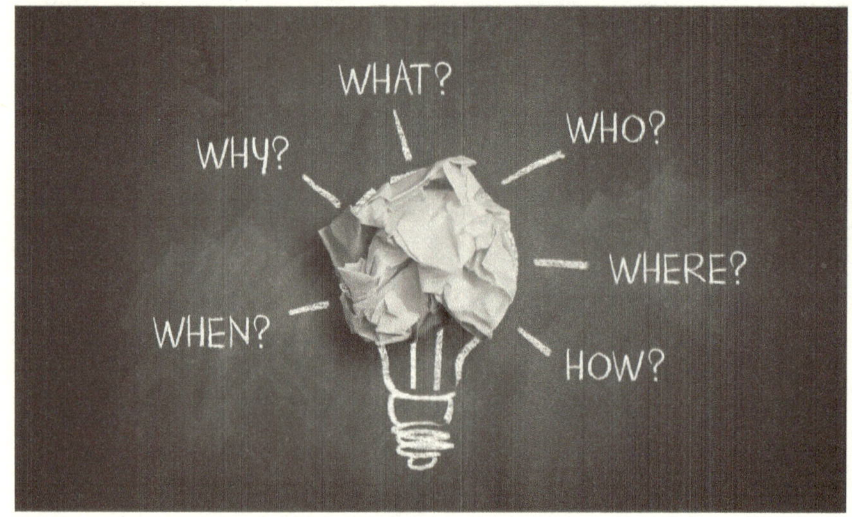

The 5 Ws of Journalism
iStock.com/http://www.fotogestoeber.de

The tool of having an analytical mindset helps spotting assumptions that we have about situations that are not true. Sometimes we block our growth because we assume something to be good, yet it really may be bad, and we need to spot the fallacy–the lie. Usually when we ask ourselves what the right thing to do is and we do the opposite, chances are we are justifying it with a lie to get some perceived pleasure out of it. It rarely is benefiting us though.

Robert Kegan and Lisa Laskow Lahey explored in their book [54] how sometimes we may hold deep lies about things which prevents us from growing. Those lies that we assume as true keep us rooted in fear to move forward, and usually the real case is hardly as dangerous as we fear.

We must know why sometimes we find it difficult to change, and by analyzing it we may spot the reason. We may assume, for instance, that if we change dreadful things may happen, or a protection we had gets lost, but usually when we test those assumptions they turn out to be untrue. By embracing a positive change with all our hearts we bring up all its goodness and dispel the deep unconscious reasons we falsely believe to avoid the change.

There is a concept in scriptures that sometimes we have a little voice that tells us in our brain to do bad things–or simply pushes us with argumentations to do a wrong thing –and tries to entice us with fallacious reasoning. Usually it is a mystical knowledge that this voice is meant to challenge us so that we exert effort and go beyond our current limitations.

Adam and Eve are the canonical example of being enticed with lies. The serpent would be that voice persuading them to eat the forbidden fruit. To achieve this the serpent is said to have pushed Eve against the fruit first so that she would be less afraid to eat it afterwards. She thought it was forbidden to touch the fruit too, besides what she knew about not eating it. Adam had told her that touching the fruit was also forbidden for good intentions– so that she would have extra protection–yet it was done with a lie. When touching it and nothing happening, Eve assumed that eating the fruit would be okay too, but at the end it brought only death.

Lying is dangerous for others and for ourselves. We must always be in the side of truth–with the exception maybe of maintaining peace in our home or avoiding injustices coming from others like would be theft or physical harm. We should always be as close to the truth as possible.

We must always analyze ourselves to spot those hidden lies that persuade us to do something that is not correct; or that try to persuade us to avoid a positive change that we want to do. When we use simple logic and analyze the issue, we rapidly realize that what we thought of the bad thing as good may be simply a bad impression, and when we fear that the good may bring us harm it is probably a false assumption. Simply doing the right thing and stopping and thinking with questions and answers in case of doubt is the best way to spot inconsistencies or fallacies that we may assume to be true. When spotting them we will be in reality with ourselves.

We must never let false fears or false assumptions deter us from doing the right thing. In the end all will be good, we will be good, and everything with exceedingly high probability will end up having all the good outcomes destined for us. Our effort and persistence keeping our chosen path and walking it with righteousness, boldness, and trust will make it true for years to come.

12

Time to enjoy

Who is rich? He who rejoices in his lot, as it is said: "When you eat of the labor of your hands, you are happy and all is well with you." – Ethics of the fathers 4, 1

Joy in our own daily lives

Western society has happiness as an ultimate goal, money as a means for it, and reality cannot be further from the truth. Depressions are at an all-time high, and among the most affordable we could even dare to say there is sometimes acute dissatisfaction.

Should we say poverty is the solution? Certainly poverty is very harsh–and at times it is equated with death. We should be always joyful with all we have, but poverty is not only that there is less money than another. Sometimes we talk about extreme situations without any form of living, and totally living out of charity.

Dissatisfaction sometimes does not come nor even in being rich, nor being poor, nor being middle class. It comes with a lack of purpose; a lack of something to do that fills us; and ultimately a lack of enjoying the fruits of our labors.

Today I can tell that I have helped people–poor people– in dire situations. One was looking for a job with his spouse, and the other person with a daughter and a wife forced to live in the streets. I can tell living in the streets is an extremely challenging situation to feel joy. What was worrying them the most though was not their dire situation per se; what worried them was not being able to provide for their kids.

Ultimate joy is mostly related with a state of gratitude and sharing–we have and we provide for others. Ultimate joy is also related with trust. We trust all will be good, the Creator will provide, or we just trust that our endeavors will turn out a success.

The art of being joyful is difficult to master at times. Can we be joyful when we have a dire situation? Can we be joyful when we are stricken by illness, G-d forbid? Yes, not everybody will be able to acquire a state of joy, but the truth is that optimally we should always have a state of joy.

There are different kinds of joy [55]: we have the broadest general joy which is manifested in its fullest sense; pure joy of being with others; an awe inspiring joy also manifested in dancing; a more worldly joy that manifests strongly and comes as a wave to later dissipate; enjoyment of something specific which could be a thing or an activity; a prideful joy seen, for instance, in a parent with his children; a deeper joy connected to an inner peace or a yearning to a life of meaning; a joy coming unexpectedly; an uplifting joy

coming from some conscious realization; and diferent kinds
of joys that are expressed through a cry, a shout, or a
sudden singing, dancing, or cheering.

The way to manifest joy are various, but the need to be
joyful in all that we do is paramount to maintain a happy
and healthy life–overall when we have worked hard to earn
our living.

We should dedicate a day weekly to feel joy and be joyful
with family and friends by bringing tasty food, uplifting
drinks, good companion, beautiful decoration, or even
good clothing. At the very least we should dedicate the day
to stop working, appreciate our bounty, and enjoy it.

Special times during the year are also propitious to have
joy. In scripture it is prompted to have joy in the
recollection seasons, which would be spring for Shavuot
when barely is recollected, or fall for Succoth where the
wheat has dried and it can be picked up. In general they are
propitious times where we assess the produce of our hard
work and it is proper to enjoy the days with celebration,
sharing it with family and friends. One way to do it is
thanking G-d for the yield trusting that we will receive more
yield in the future; and simply enjoying rightfully the
material pleasures, moments, and activities that we earned
so meritoriously from our hard work.

In the book [56] of Mike Wiking, from the Happiness
Research Institute, he points out how Danish people have a
sense of happiness by enjoying life and varied moments
with the aid of being actively focused on having joy. They
carefully prepare the celebrations, nice calm moments, or
any crafted situation. From it we learn that the use of
decorations, guests, and a lot of minute details help to

introduce joy in our lives even in areas as seemly detached as would be our work environment.

Having joy in all that we do is a key ingredient to succeed. A work, a project, or any activity having been done with joy brings hormones that calm stress, induces focus, and promotes this activity to be done with a high rate of success.

Although the science of the hormone interplay that happens during joyful moments is complex, we can deduce from various research [57] that good nutrients and healthy activity help arriving to these joyful situations. We need joy in our labor to perform it with satisfaction and success. Among other activities to induce joyful moments at work are: breaking tasks into smaller tasks and mark them when done; finding variation among routine; some creativity; sun light; staying positive; socializing; giving; and being grateful.

It is not easy to find joy in everything, but being joyful is a personal task that must be achieved with all our attention. We must try and shift situations to arrive to a state of joy while we do them. We can work on what to focus on like: little aide from decoration; our tools for work; our clothing; lighting; health; sport; energy; beauty; or even the most insignificant details that, while others may not care, makes us do something with passion and joy.

Having joy is a choice, and we can choose to have joy or not. Deciding to have joy may include things that brings us joy, elements to do something with joy, and also a state of mind of trust and conviction that all will be right and good so that we do our tasks with joy.

To start with right now I chose to go to a famous coffee shop to write this piece. I was wondering how to inspire myself to write this with an amount of joy worthy of the lecture. So that is my joy. Now, I notice the minute details, the music, the light, the decoration, and the serenity. There is an indescribable serenity amidst a huge amount of chatter—as if we were in the loft of a mountain refuge after a long day of skiing.

Coffee shop with natural light

I drove to a parking lot full of cars and almost without effort a car left just when four cars were looking in front of me. I set out to enjoy this morning writing this part, and I visualized where I wanted to sit, what I wanted to take, and the good atmosphere I was expecting to have. It is true that living in Barcelona the nice weather is a given, nevertheless, today is outstandingly good: clear skies, a perfect weather, and a perfect breeze.

I did not know exactly how to inspire myself today to have joy, but for this I chose the utmost time of the year that a Jew is commanded to have joy. Now is Succoth, the festivity of dwelling in a booth for a week enjoying meals in the view of the stars, the sky, and the breeze. This is a time for joy, and a time to enjoy it with others.

When I came the queue to buy something here was outstanding, and I saw that all the coffee shop was full. I was thinking for an instant that I would need to take my breakfast home instead of enjoying it in the coffee shop. Somehow I just kept waiting while in the right moment the table I visualized before me freed on the spot. Today it was meant to be a day full of joy.

Joy that all will be good

When I was in university I remember I fell incredibly low, a lifestyle that was not proper of myself. The studies were falling behind like they did in the last year of high school where I had that little incident with the pool. I remember I did not know how to get out of that mess. I needed money, but I had to stop working to do it all.

Like when I was in high school suddenly I had a deep conversation with a family friend I barely knew. He was a business co-owner that with his brother used to invite my family from time to time to nice meals. Conversing with him was the usual chat we did to catch up on what we were doing. I told him I used to work on the weekends as a waiter in a famous restaurant that the then King of Spain ate once on the coast, but though I enjoyed it a lot it was taking a toll. After some good advice from him and from that moment on I just stopped working on the weekends, and decided that I did not know how to get out of that mess of expensive tuitions, yet I needed time to study all. So, I just set myself to just do the right thing, and hope for the best.

When we are trapped—and when we are not—there is a little "*Secret*", and that is called hope. We do not know exactly how things will work out nor what circumstances lead us to our goals, but when we put our hope on the above—G-d—things work out in marvelous ways.

Once I heard that if you desire something deeply you can get what you want. I do not know exactly what we want, but sometimes there is mercy in not giving us all we want—otherwise we would get into troubles.

I once set out to eat in an extremely expensive restaurant, those that you reserve well in advance, and costs a nice amount of money, but I paid for it, and tried it once. The song that played first when I sat there still resonates on my mind. "You can't always get what you want, but if you try sometime, well, you will find that you get what you need."

And this is the motto. All we do always happens for a greater good. All we experience, all we live is exactly crafted so that it pushes us to do what we must do, to receive what we must receive, and to perfect ourselves in this world for years and years to come.

We do not always get what we want, but we must trust we will get what we need. If our desires come from a source of good, usually what we want is entwined with what we need. At that moment we must trust with all our hearts that only this good will come out from all our experiences and tests.

We saw before that there are different kinds of joy, joy in music and dancing, joy in a moment, all-encompassing joy in general–and also joy of the unexpected. In the Red Sea crossing all the people of Israel were scared. There were the Egyptians coming to kill them on one side, and the unsurmountable Red Sea on the other. We find that they divided in three types: some wanted to fight the Egyptians; others wanted to surrender; and the third group just prayed for deliverance. The reason nothing happened is because there was not enough trust.

The case of Nachshon ben Aminadav is a case to emulate. While some wanted to surrender when followed by the Egyptians at the Red Sea; others wanted to attack; and others prayed without full conviction and without much success. Nachshon ben Aminadav, from the tribe of Judah and ancestor of most famous kings like David, decided then to jump into the sea. He knew that G-d would deliver them, so he started walking and walking. The water started getting into his neck in stormy conditions–enough to drown him at any moment and kill him in the depths of the sea. People must had been baffled. "What is he doing?" "Has he lost his mind?" Moses was praying for G-d's deliverance, and G-d said to him at that moment.

"My beloved ones are drowning in the stormy seas, and you are standing and praying?"

"Master of the world, what am I to do?" said Moses

"You lift your staff and spread your hand over the seas, which will split, and Israel will come into the sea upon dry land."

We cannot always jump into the stormy sea with full conviction, but what we can do is to increase the conviction that things will be good, and that a deliverance and a splitting of the sea will happen when we most need it. We may not always get what we want, but if we try sometime, well, we just might find that we get what we need. Nachshon exemplified this trust by jumping into the sea and showing in the name of all Israelites that there was trust–a pure trust that all will be good, and all will work out in a way that even our most crafted ideas are not able to foresee [58].

In Succoth there is a special command, meaning that if you do it you show your devotion and walk the path of the upright: the special command is to have joy. Indeed we are to know that these days the central command is to have joy. We invite others to a meal, friends, or just guests. I found a man with his family a few months ago that was evicted from his home and lost his job. After helping them tomorrow I am inviting them to have a meal in an all-you-can-eat nice restaurant.

This is our lot. Sometimes we have to get joy in the worst conditions of the world–and this joy only comes when we know that the Master of the world performs miracles in the hardest of times. For instance, Succoth ended and immediately afterwards seems that joy disappeared in an instant. Israel was savaged with the worst heinous acts a human can fathom when after of a music festival the unthinkable happened. Women abused and killed, hundreds murdered, and the wickedness of some human beings put in display without a modicum of shame.

There are three ways to get joy under adverse situations: we can accept the situation we are faced and try to get as much joy as we can despite the situation; we can decide to be positive and expect the situation to change by having joy; or we can choose to have genuine joy by understanding that what is happening is for our ultimate good.

Everything that happens to us is for the ultimate good. We do not see the bigger picture; we do now know where our soul was in previous lives; and we do not know how what is happening is leading us to the ultimate good, but there is a truth–and that is that G-d is good. All that happens in the world, even what seems the most horrendous of acts unimaginable, is done by His servants, exacts justice, and leads always to good. Not meaning that the perpetrators are left without justice served to them.

This world is created with free will, and we are those responsible for choosing right or choosing wrong. Not everything is disclosed to us, but if we look carefully we may be able to assess that everything that happened to us was meant to get good. And when we see it we can only enjoy; because when we see it we can only feel good. When we see it we can see that all that happened, all that happens, and all that will happen is crafted so that we and all grow to joy, and that we emulate G-d's attributes in this world: good will, wisdom, understanding, knowledge, love, strength, mercy, endurance, humility, creativity, and joy– lots of joy.

War are not times of joy, misplaced fear is not, and not all moments are conducive to joy. Sometimes we must reach deeper: deeper on our souls; deeper on our purpose; and deeper on our hearts [59]. A prophet needed to be joyful in order to receive prophecy. Since all that comes from G-d is good, even the direst predictions had to be good. He had to be joyful to get information from G-d, and this joy had to be attached with the realization that all is ultimately good.

Once, some sages were exploring the destroyed ruins of the Jewish temple in Jerusalem, and a fox was running on the most sacred part where only the high priest was allowed to enter just once in the entire year. The sages started crying while one started screaming with joy. When they asked him why he was so joyful, he quoted: "Therefore, for your sake Zion shall be plowed as a field, and Jerusalem shall become rubble, and the Temple Mount as the high places of a forest." He was quoting a prophecy that was being fulfilled in front of their eyes. Seeing this fulfilled meant that the predictions were true, so the joy that is predicted in the future will be also true.

A glass is broken in a Jewish wedding so that an acknowledgment is made that if we behave good, in the future we will always experience the ultimate joy, the joy that all will be good, our lives will end up good, and G-d will accept us with the ultimate good–to experience pure joy, and to experience pure truth.

The habit of being good

The key of growth is not only growing ourselves, but to share this growth with all the people around. We are part of a bigger world, and we must make our mark. Everybody has a different part. The wisdom we are going to show now certainly can be used very actively now. It is not only our own growth that matters, but the growth we make with those around.

13

Show to others

Do not withhold good from its rightful recipients, when you have the power to do it.
(Proverbs 3:27)

The power of observation

The best way to ingrain our faculties is when we show them to others. When we grow and when we learn, we acquire certain traits and certain abilities that others do not have. People crave for truth and righteousness, but where there is lacking we must be the torch–the holders of these virtues.

If we have others in mind while we grow, while we learn, and while we practice, all these abilities and improvements we set out to do get done with more care. In the end our work is not isolated to ourselves. People are thirsty for growth, and where there is an example we will have followers. We will have people that have other problems and are also fighting to improve. It is then when all our knowledge will need to be divulged. Our progress will need to be kept in check, because then we will become role models.

We must learn things having in mind that one day somebody will want to know about these things. Maybe someday we see somebody in need of key advice; so we must be ready to understand others, to read their needs, and to say just what they need to thrive and to keep advancing in life.

Teaching is one of the best ways to learn. When we teach, we force ourselves to clarify our minds. All that we want to convey must be truly clear to us because we will be asked questions, and we will need to be understood. When we learn knowing that this knowledge and wisdom will be used, not only by ourselves, but also by others, we learn with more acumen. Usually then is when we start getting key points. What are the key points of this teaching? How would we explain it? How would it be used? How it connects to other teachings?

When we learn it is good that we classify the information into different types. Sometimes we get some piece of information and we relate it to something it belongs to. This is the best way to keep something we learn stored in our memories: relating it with something else. Is this information talking about life? About business? About myself? About the workings of the world? Relating the information to some theme or some other information helps our brain to retain it and to be able to extract it conveniently later on.

Showing to others not only means teaching information—it also means teaching about life. Doing acts of kindness by helping people in need is one of the pillars that sustains the world. We can give money to somebody in need; do acts of kindness by visiting the sick; helping others in need; or giving time and teaching others. When we know that we can help somebody, and this requires some time to teach something, all this time is an act of righteousness. Guiding somebody, teaching something, or just being there when somebody is in need are all notable examples of kindness.

During our lives we become good at somethings, and we learn certain traits or abilities that others do not have. Sometimes when we show others how to proceed, how things are done, or show them the right thing to do, we unite with the world in a way. We show that we are us, but also that we are part of a people. We have a union with more things than ourselves–our spouse, our families, our friends, our communities, our neighbors, our loved ones, our entire being, and G-d.

When we show to others we make the community grow, our fellows grow, and all our close ones grow with us. Usually when we study a profession, a craftsmanship, or an ability, we are not only good by reading about it–we need somebody to explain it to us. We also need to explain it to others–to show how it is done. Giving an example is one of the best tools to finally connect all the dots and to understand in a heartfelt manner what we are being shown. We must always keep doing what we do in a right way. Not only for ourselves, but because unbeknown to us we also become role models for other people. When we learn, we not only learn by improving our own skills. A lot of times we learn by observing others, and others learn by observing us.

In the brain there is a special mechanism in which neurons replicate what other persons do to create empathy. When neurons activate this mechanism the neurons performing this activity are called mirror neurons. [60] Mirror neurons activity play a pivotal role in reproducing the actions seen in others in our own brain. The job they do is empathizing with a situation.

Initially it was thought that mirror neurons function was more motor like. When we see somebody dancing, if we are dancers for instance, we can relate with that person as if we were dancing too while we see their moves, because we rehearse in our brains in a way what we see with our own eyes. The brain, by the position the dancers are having and such while dancing, knows or relates to other moments when we ourselves danced in an analogous way, and starts feeling, sort to speak, as if we were dancing too. This applies to any other activity we are familiar too.

Mirror neurons activity is what helps us learn by imitation or observation. It also helps us to understand other people's actions, feelings, or emotions by playing in our brain what is the whole process that in reality the other person must be feeling or doing. The mirror name comes from that. Somebody performs an action that we are interested in for some reason, and neurons behave like mirror neurons, and start replicating, or better yet, activating a similar activity to the one we are seeing, and that we already did in the past before. It will reactivate the activity or feeling in our brains and all its related processes, with the exception that it will not translate it into real actions without our consent.

Sometimes in certain situations mirror neurons even dare to replicate the action as a whole. When we yawn in front of other people, more usually than not if they are not aware that we may be testing them, they will yawn back. Sometimes, for instance, I hesitate coughing in public when I need it, but usually when I cannot resist the reply is that some people choose to cough immediately afterwards I do, and a small trend ensues.

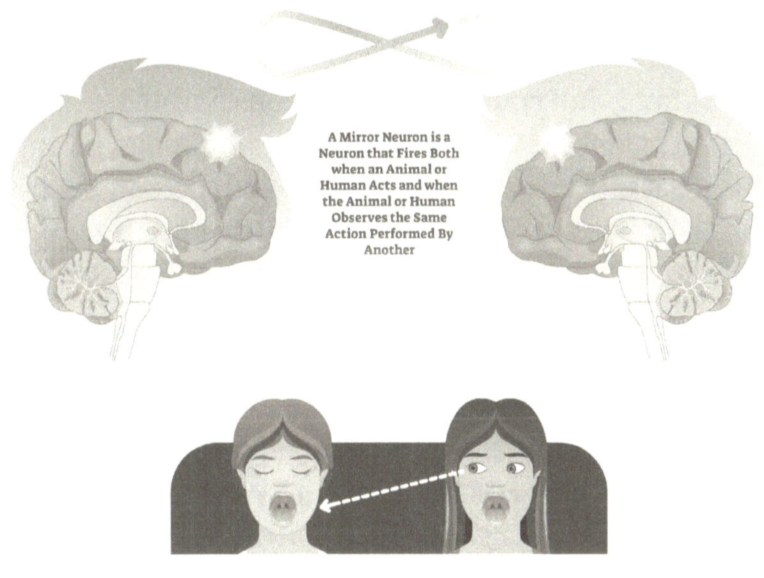

Mirror neurons in action
iStockphoto.com/VectorMine

When neurons act in a mirror way, some inhibitory neurons also activate so that they usually limit the activity to only feelings, and not actual movements or real actions from our body. Mirror neurons is called in reality to the double role neurons play. They activate normally in ourselves to do something, and they activate too, yet more inhibited, when we see others doing also that same thing.

That is why our behaviors matter. If we are smiling, people smile back. If we start running in the street as if running from a danger, chances are other people will start running too–just in case. If we start laughing, other people will start laughing too–even though they have no idea what we are laughing about.

We are social by nature, but it turns out that our brains are also attuned to what other people do. What we do affects others, and consciously or unconsciously we have a tendency to imitate, or at least to relate and replay in our brains what others are doing. If we go with certain people, we like it or not their customs and habits will start to permeate, because our nature is to relate and imitate from the very strata of our brains.

It is our responsibility to behave good; to be role models to others; and moreover to actively help others improve, grow, and show them how it is done–in case they are interested, and they are attuned for it. We do not know when somebody is activating their mirror neurons on us, nor how what we do affects other persons. That is why being ready to act always good is a way to improve beyond ourselves.

Teaching others and showing others our abilities, counsel, or any other information others may use is a way to grow. We improve our loved ones, our surroundings, and directly or indirectly the world. What we do causes an effect on others, and others in turn also teach it others the same way. When the actions prove to be good, beneficial, and right, they mark an impression that go beyond transient trends or fashions of the time–we grow and make the world grow with us beyond our wildest expectations.

The power of words

Every day of our lives we wake up and use speech to communicate. We use words to understand other people; to understand about what is going on in the world. We use words in our particular language, and usually we use words to speak, words to hear, words to write, and words to read. What we may not know is that words are also used to create. G-d created the world with ten utterances. No other tool was used, just words.

When we use words we not only communicate, but we also change reality. Every word that we say has an effect on the listener and in ourselves. The brain–our brain–hears the words that we say, and as we already know they are not always processed in a conscious manner. When we perceive the world, we have an idea about it, but when we put its details into words it becomes real, describable, finite, and concrete: the concept takes a real form.

Every time that we talk we communicate to others and to ourselves; we let our mind know not only what we think, but also how it has to feel. The classical example is when we say negative things just for the fun of it. "I cannot do it." "This is impossible." Or worst yet, we utter negative statements of what we will do in the future. Every word that we say has a tremendous power–more power than most of us give credit for.

Talking positively not only helps us to do things better, but changes reality itself. Sometimes we may say. "Oh, but it's the truth." If we believe something is the truth, overall, an attitude or a feeling, chances are we will transform into reality those same very words we utter, be it that they were originally true or not.

Jacob, when he was accused by Laban to have stolen his idolatrous figure, was so convinced and assured that it was not his fault that it was stolen—nor of his family—that he said, "The one with whom you find your gods shall not live." [61] Little he knew that Rachel, his most beloved wife, had stolen the figure to protect his father from using it. What happened next is that Rachel died later while giving birth to her second child.

The words that we say to ourselves and that we say to others can cause a profound effect. Every word matters, and just by wishing good morning to another person, talking positively, giving courage, or even looking at situations with hope and positive speaking we create the reality and the environment for those same very things that we say to become true.

Words are a double-edged sword. We can encourage people to do the most unimaginable things, and even into ourselves; or we can destroy others and destroy ourselves with just uttering words. Gossip—or ill speaking of somebody—is one of the most destructive tools that exist to destroy a person's reputation, or just damage it enough to destroy some of the success. What we must also realize is that talking negatively about somebody not only destroys the other person in a way, but it also destroys us.

When we criticize somebody or a group of people, even small, an evil accusatory angel is created that has permission to also utter a judgment on ourselves [62]. The accusatory angel creates a scrutiny of our wrong doings that forces a premature sentence in heaven before we even regret the wrong doings we committed from our hearts–or even before we try to change. The sentences proposed by the accusatory angels are usually crueler than the one G-d would propose for us–such is the destructive power of negative words.

Positive words achieve the opposite: unity and resolve. When the things we want to say are said with care, measuring our words, without slander nor ridiculing somebody either present in the conversation or not, we achieve an effective communication: we empower others to listen to us, and others open up to us in turn.

Example of positive words
iStockphoto.com/bankrx

Once, I saw a famous television show–the only episode I watched maybe from this show–where two groups of people were competing with each other to have the better marketing ideas. One group was criticizing each other for not performing better pointing out their faults and almost always competing–mostly among themselves–in a very destructive way. The other group just encouraged each other to give the best of their abilities. They always were being positive and having joy while doing it. We do not need to say which group outperformed the other–just to clarify, the latter.

We must not lie and be always positive. Indeed the power of words is such that when we commit to do something, even if it is in words, we should do it exactly as we say to encourage this pattern of commitment in our brains. This elevates our reputation of trustworthy persons in others, and most importantly in ourselves. It is necessary to be accurate in our wordings. "I will do it", is not the same than "I will try" nor than "I may do it." We must not criticize nor use negative speech unnecessarily, yet we must also be careful that what we say is always accurate and true. Being honest and truthful is one of the most beloved qualities to succeed as persons and in any endeavor we pursue.

Our words matter, what we say to others matters, and how truthful we are and how we follow through with what we say or promise also matter. A computer program is a set of instructions that determine very clearly what the task will do, and how it will behave. Sure, a program does not have neither the ability to empathize; neither to withhold sensitive information on their own accord; nor to communicate willingly with meaningful positive words. But we must realize that, like a program, what we utter with our mouths has a concrete effect on the world.

If we meditate about a concept or idea while repeating it concisely, precisely, and periodically, we may connect with this concept–and even make it into reality in a way. Of course, the limits are obvious, and worst of all, the ill-conceived desires or ideas can divert us or not be good in any way. The use of meditation for positive habits–or for achieving righteous things that we want–can help us internalize attitudes or behaviors that we want and need to have in our lives to succeed.

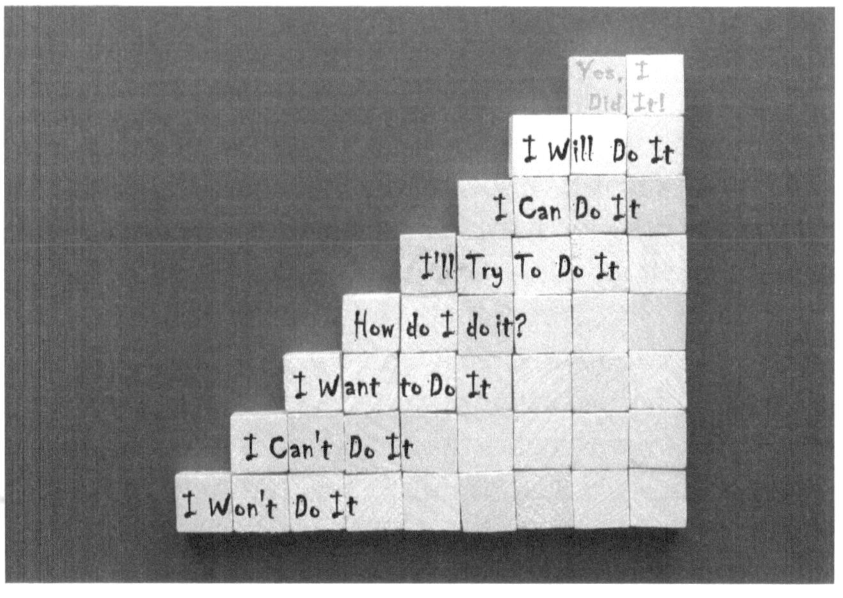

Words that we say, meditate, or think affect what we do
iStockphoto.com/ogichobanov

Being truthful is an art. Sometimes, for the sake of peace, or to protect us from somebody that wants to do us harm, we may alter the truth. Certainly these are valid moments where we can lie–or sugar-coat things. Being truthful in other matters is a habit that we must check and constantly practice. This way, slowly but surely, we become more reliable and more trusted by others and by ourselves. We cannot show things to others if our words are of little value, but we can pierce with words if what we say is trusted and true.

We can avoid talking if we will slander somebody. There is usually no benefit in talking negatively about people–nor even the supposed benefit of learning a lesson. At times, though, when we prevent theft, real harm, or even disclose honest necessary information to an affianced–future husband or wife–it becomes then a good thing to talk openly about people.

The habit of positive speaking is a habit to be created by looking at ourselves and catching what we say during the day. We ought to train to be careful what we promise with our mouths so that we comply and we do exactly as we say. We must be careful that we are honest with others and with ourselves. Saying always the truth does not mean that we have to say everything we think or know, just that when we say something we must always say the truth very accurately and with care.

Let us cultivate the habit of guarding our words so that when we say something, it is not only normally something true, but reliable and sincere. People then will hardly have any doubt that when we say something we mean it, and the words that we utter are always true and good.

14

The lessons of the past

Remember the days of yore, understand the years of generation after generation. Ask your father and he will relate it to you, your elders and they will tell you. (Deuteronomy 32:7)

The lessons from others' experience

Wisdom can be general, but it can also be very particular to our path of growth. Sometimes we are engaged in activities or certain situations that require specific wisdom that is used in that area. Some wisdom must be applied to certain circumstances and must be inferred, but people who have lived similar situations than what we need to know can give us this distilling knowledge right away. The reason is the details are very similar, and we relate immediately if indeed this wisdom and all its details are valid and true.

For that reason, in life we must acquire wisdom from people, from our family, from friends, or from strangers.

Any encounter or advice we get from people that already lived similar experiences or warn us about future situations we may encounter is very valuable. Experience from other people is a true heartfelt wisdom. It is an application of wisdom where the lessons we can extract can be applied with a lot of detail to our current situations.

Wisdom from history is good, but history is not always transmitted accurately. Some of it is fully validated, but the conclusions and the lessons learnt from them are not necessarily precise. Taking lessons from people that lived the situations and can tell us genuinely what they felt and how it was is a good source of information to get a real-life experience. We can learn lessons of what right mindsets they had, little details that may had been determinant for success, or attitudes or things that were essential for them and may have been later ignored.

We can learn lessons from parents, friends, biography books, stories being told by others, and from people we meet in our lives. We can learn from people that speak truth about what they lived and explain what the outcomes were, and what they learnt. All of them are a good source to get lessons and minimize mishaps. They will help us grow faster towards our goals. It is good too to have them in store for future events that we may encounter.

We must look for genuine information, reliable sources, and truthful outcomes. We must get used to the habit of extracting lessons from the past; from events that already happened and got to a conclusion. This way we can understand better how it ended up that way. Habituating ourselves to extract lessons from everything is necessary to be better next time; to behave always good; to adapt fast to situations we may not have experienced before; and in general to be very skilled at acquiring valuable wisdom for life.

Listening is a great tool to get lessons from others. Usually, when we let people speak, they tell us what they felt; what was valuable to them; what lessons they learnt; what are the assumptions they had; and how the experience validated or showed them otherwise. Listening hence is an important habit to acquire wisdom. Being humble and hearing what other persons have to say, what other people experienced, and what they have to tell us about anything is important to acquire a valuable wisdom that we will carry all our lives.

The path of everybody is unique, and we cannot traverse all the situations that we may encounter, but others have and can tell us about its result. This wisdom is valuable because a lot of times, even if we did not live the exact experience, we will find similar situations where we can apply the lessons extracted from others. By learning from others past or what they lived we can also infer patterns that repeat themselves and that we ourselves can observe by the similar stories we read or that we are being told.

Being humble and listening to others counsel and wisdom is paramount to be ourselves wise. We save a lot of trouble along the way, and we can get nuggets of wisdom from everybody. Wisdom at times is very particular. That one person is more intelligent or that a generation has more scientific knowledge does not mean one is beyond the experiences of others' past, nor that the way things were done in the past are always worse than the present. Not all things are correlated, and wisdom is applied in very different manners and ways. Any experience that somebody lived can give us details on what to do or what to avoid. When we stop acquiring wisdom from others or other generation because we believe it of no value we are doomed to repeat unnecessary mistakes that may be hard to recover from.

The wisdom we acquire must be personal. We have general wisdom, but the wisdom of others that we encounter through life is wisdom that is usually meant for us. If we ignore that wisdom, or choose not to listen to it, chances are that we may learn it the hard way. The lessons we extract from history or from others must be inferred by us. We will be told the lessons learned, but we must always go beyond and infer ourselves from the story being told what lessons we do extract from them.

In summary, when we are in a situation that we want to do right or we find that we are not knowledgeable enough, we should learn from people who experienced these situations before. Getting advice from other persons, reading biographies, knowing what worked for them, and what did not is paramount to get a right foot in every endeavor we do. It is crucial that we learn to extract patterns that repeat themselves. If we are not sure we can test it against a similar story. Is the pattern consistent? Does one thing lead always to the other thing?

We should be very skillful in listening to others; extracting nuggets of knowledge from anything we read or being told; and extract its patterns. The lessons are meant for us, so it is okay that we focus on what is of interest to us. How this applies to me? Why this maybe important in the future? This way we will be more confident and secure in all that we do. We will already know which path to go.

We must be absorbers of wisdom from all sources we are privy to, even if we think that our brain memory capacity is limited during our lifetime–which it is not the case [63].

The lessons from our own past

Our past, we like it or not, is full of lessons. Every event that we have lived, every success, every failure, and every mishap have in it lessons on what to do and what to avoid. A lot of lessons from other people give us wisdom, lessons from our own past give us self-wisdom. Our path is our own, though shared in a lot of moments. Sometimes we must learn lessons that are uniquely applied to us; lessons that are nice and prone to repeat; lessons that we felt ashamed that we needed them; lessons on why we reached to certain situations; or lessons on how to outperform in certain moments.

All the events we live are at times crafted so that we extract lessons from them: a hardship, something we craved for, or a momentary success out of the ordinary. It is an efficient way of living reviewing our past and understanding what we can use from it so that the next time we are in a similar situations we do the right thing.

Sometimes we are blinded by something we pursue and we fall again and again; we are smashed to a wall and we do not know why. A lot of times only a little sincere introspection with ourselves will tell us the truth. We just have to check the situations that we did not succeed against the situations that we did succeed. With honesty we will extract easily what are the underlying reasons we ended up one way or the other.

Life is full of lessons: from stories known from our family and friends; from books; or from things that we did and experienced. Every moment we live usually has lessons embedded in them. While living we should explore and take notes of lessons in life that we learn. In the beginning we may be a little clumsy, but with experience we will start extracting the right lessons.

Lesson embedded in dice
iStockphoto.com/Fokusiert

We can always have a notebook and a pencil available and write down significant lessons we encounter during the day. We can also do it at night and take notes of the lessons that would apply to our lives. We would be surprised how important some lessons are later on in the future, and a good source for them can be found embedded in our own past.

Extracting lessons from our past seems difficult after all the experiences we had, but we do not need to review every moment we remember. We just have to do it by issue –or by something that may be of interest to us. For instance, when we want to learn how to behave better or succeed at something, besides future wisdom from others, chances are that we already have experienced it ourselves from past attempts. It is wise to review all the situations where we were in a similar set up than the one we want to extract lessons from, and analyze why we succeeded or why we did not. What was our mindset? Was it correct? We should extract lessons and see if we did all that we had to do, or if we kept doing the same mistakes that were affecting the outcomes.

The key to improve is extracting lessons from experiences we lived. It is good to analyze what we did in the past regarding certain issues, and what key lessons standout from those experiences. How did others perform? What did they do that was key and maybe we did not? Also, the other way around, What key moments did we do better at something that others did not? What were the key elements that we were doing that granted success?

Extracting lessons from the past is an exercise of observance. When we do something there are patterns that consistently use to lead to failure, and patterns that lead to success. We should be careful that we extract the right lessons and not take the wrong conclusions or associations. It is good that we know what real success means, and if this success was achieved doing the right thing. If we have clarity on both, chances are we will understand always what are the key elements that veers a situation towards one outcome or the other.

Sometimes we are the best examples of what happens when we do the right thing or we do the wrong thing. We should understand all the moments that we did not act correctly; what their final outcomes were; and how we could avoid ever repeating reaching to those situations. Making an accounting of what we did is a good way to improve ourselves. If it was good or bad; right or wrong; how it could have been done better; how we should deeply avoid doing what was bad; or how we should continue repeating what was good and right in the future.

Our lives need constant polishing, and only we do know what we lived in the past, what exactly is that we did good or we did wrong, how we can perfect it, and what lessons we can take so that we do it better next time.

American football professional players review in their locker rooms how they performed in the first part of their games. During the week they and their teams play video cuts of their past game in special all twenty-two field view cameras, and watch games cuts from the coming opponent team. By learning what key elements were done right consistently they can be reinforced. By learning what key elements were hampering their progress they can be avoided. This is done in all categories of professional football, sports, and any competitive set up–only that we do compete against ourselves.

To reach to higher levels of success every time–and to be always at the peak of our own performance or progress–we need to be self-aware of our own situations. We need to be good at extracting lessons and writing them down or remembering them. We will progress very fast if we are aware of the valuable lessons from all the key events we live and we have lived in the past. The key is thinking, How does this benefit me? What can we learn from this? What conclusion did we learnt from that? Is it a valid conclusion? Did we extract the core lesson that will help us?

We should be honest with ourselves if we want to extract the right lessons of things. Sometimes we fail and it is difficult to recognize our mistakes, but more often than not there are lessons that are embedded in them, and tell us what we did correctly, what we did not, or what we believed was right and it turn out to be wrong–or the other way around. Only being honest with ourselves and accepting our mistakes we can truly improve and avoid future pitfalls.

Only we do have the events in our heads; only we do have the details, what we felt, what we thought, or what we knew. It is our responsibility to extract lessons from our own experiences and see the details that we should repeat or we should avoid. The tools for repentance are an exploration of our past, analyzing what we did right and wrong, knowing and understanding why the wrong was bad, and committing from our hearts to not repeat this wrong anymore.

The opposite is true. We do have values and abilities that sometimes need an exploration so that we can understand how to get the most out of them. What did we do when things worked out okay? What was the situation when we outperformed, did good, or felt well? Can it be repeated? By knowing and learning from our own past we can walk unflinchingly into our own the future.

Life is full of lessons, but usually what we encounter and what we live are lessons meant for us, so we should focus on what key points that we learn from something do relate to us, or can help us now or in the future in any way. Habituating ourselves to do this is a good way to avoid mistakes and to walk with success. The advice is to acquire wisdom from events that we live that may contain valuable lessons and may be applied to us. We should apply them to our interests, to our future situations, and keep them around in case one day they might be useful to us.

In case of complex situations we should wait till the event passes to extract its meaningful lessons. When the event has concluded we can see the lessons with its full perspective and its implications. Extracting lessons from a distance gives us the bird's eye view. History is an example of that. We can only extract the lessons when we have unbiased information of most of the meaningful events. When they have passed, we can deduce what led to what; what was related to other things; and all in all what key moments, key situations, or key attitudes moved things one way or another.

Let us do at least one accounting of our lives: what we did right, what we did wrong, how we can improve, and what key lessons we can take so that we can walk faster, stronger, and wiser next time. By taking lessons from the past and from the present we can apply these lessons in the future. The lessons can be introspected on our own or can be hinted by other people telling us how to correct our ways, but the end result is always the same—a righteous path, a paved road, and success.

15

Be the head and not the tail

*G-d shall place you as a head and not as a tail;
you shall be only above and you shall not be
below–if you hearken to the commandments of
G-d, your G-d, that I command you today, to
observe and to perform. (Deuteronomy 28:13)*

Being the head of ourselves

When we have a clear idea of what is that we should do and have habituated to do it, we must keep steadfast to that course. Sometimes circumstances, events, or influences may push us to do things others' way, or others' thinking; we must have strong values and a strong assertiveness. Once we have clarified what we ought to do, we must persevere and head the course. It is important to not deviate nor left nor right. We must be strong and believe in ourselves and our values, and be always at the head and not at the tail of all we choose.

When we are at the head of our choices we must also watch out for new habituations–new circumstances. Sometimes small habits develop unnoticed or by influence. This must not occur if they are wrong and do not benefit us in any way. We must be vigilant and always decide what habits we want to introduce in our lives. It is paramount that we do an assessment of our actions regularly so that we spot with calmness the things that sometimes we should stop doing, or the things that would be good to do and we are not doing.

Habits are not always created with all our insights in mind. Sometimes by mere repetition of what others do, think, or simply by choosing the less tiring action, we create small habits that may not be the best ones for us. On the other hand thinking about ourselves regularly not only can spot what we do right or we do wrong, but at times it can reuse habits in better ways, make them more efficient, or right away just substitute them for something better or more righteous.

Being at the head requires an exercise of consciousness–of meditation. This, like other things, can also become a habit per se: the habit to direct our behavior; to shift and to decide what we want to do; and not to be mere spectators of all that just happens around us. We must always be at the head of how we want to respond to things, what we want to do about them, and ultimately be ourselves the ones who decide if we want to behave one way or another.

It is known, as we saw before, that it is very easy to get drifted away with who we are if we just let events and people influence us without our screening–without our consent. When we keep checking where we want to go and who we want to be, we can easily spot when something is adrift, when something is not beneficial, or simply when we are deviating. Being the head of ourselves implies a constant checking of where is our reference point. Where is that we want to go? Only then we can assess if we are deviating from our course, or if we are on track. We must always be at the head of ourselves, of our habits, and of our thoughts.

I once saw experienced drivers give an exercise on how to drive a car in difficult situations. To this end they added a skid car–a frame of slippery wheels attached to the suspension. There, some people got nervous and just thought constantly about crashing when they could not control the car–they saw themselves already crashed out of the road. The advice of the instructors was not to see oneself crashing, but simply to look ahead at the road and to visualize oneself getting out of it–regaining its control.

The lesson from this exercise is clear: sometimes we are in emergency situations and we cannot think if we have to move the driving wheel right, left, brake, or accelerate with all our might–consciously we cannot. On the other hand, if it were something we have experienced before, we would do just the right thing and the right movements without thinking. Even without experience, though, the advice to look ahead at the road; focusing and visualizing ourselves getting out of the situation; and taking back the control of the car is what unconsciously creates all the necessary movements, behaviors, and actuations that recovers the slippage of the car, and gains back its control.

We must always have in mind the control of that car–the control of our situations. We must look at the road ahead and just visualize ourselves in control of our bodies, in control of our emergency situations, and in control of our unexpected setups. Sometimes we may not be experienced; we may not have encountered some situations before, but we must see the road ahead–and we must see ourselves taking control. Then and only then we may end up doing just the right thing, just the right decision, the right move, and at the right time. By visualizing the good outcome we not only avert tragic situations, but we regain control of them, and become more experienced the next time around.

Researching the leadership of great entrepreneurs of our generation we can find one similarity: they all have a clear vision of where they want to go. No doubt that one must be endowed with the power to be able to maintain those visions, but even at the topmost of the decision chain it is hard for anyone that visualizes something that investors may not–or people around may not–to keep holding to those dreams. They nevertheless did hold–and people around them eventually followed, even if the initial reason was just to follow the boss.

When we are in the head of ourselves, given the proper opportunity, we may be bold enough to see things others cannot–and we may have a clarity others do not. Given that moment it is only in our hands to keep pushing our dreams and our visions. We can spot easily when others dissuade us out of fear, or usually because they may not see what we see.

It is clear that it is not easy to be at the topmost of the innovation chain, and our paths will lead us in different setups and environments. But the key to keep our dreams, our visions, and our paths is exemplified in key innovators from the onset of the century like could be: Steve Jobs, creator of Apple; Elon Musk, creator of Tesla, SpaceX or PayPal; or Jeff Bezos, creator of Amazon with its cloud computing, item recommendations, and technically advanced distribution robots. Their vision had been questioned from the get-go. People doubted what they dreamed or what they could do–and the pressure to quit was enormous on them–yet they followed through.

Steve Jobs was famous for pushing people beyond what they themselves thought would be possible. Sometimes designers told him something was impossible and he nevertheless replied they could do it, and prompted them to do it anyway–finding the way. On one occasion he replied, "If this would save a person's life could you make it boot faster?" He showed how many seconds would be saved in millions of people using the product, and once convinced they did it beyond expectations.

Walter Isaacson, biographer of Steve Jobs, tells us in his article written for Harvard Business Review [64] what are the key points of leadership to be emulated from Steve Jobs. He starts with focus. By focusing on the main product qualities he would just choose the core features of their product and discard all the unnecessary rest–something to be emulated overall for convoluted environments, tasks, lifestyles, or anywhere we would see this mindset fit [65].

Then he continues with simplification–making things simple does not mean making them cheaper or less valuable–on the contrary. Simplifying things properly requires a deep understanding of a thing in order to reduce it to its minimal expression correctly. As was typical in Jobs mindset, with deep understanding and work things could be reduced to its minimal expression.

I once had a teacher of computer architecture that came as a visitor to my university. Just a few of us made a class with her–and the end result was astonishing. Our resident teacher, though herself also a good teacher, was not able to express the ideas in a so simple and clear manner. The visitor was a renowned world expert, and understood the subject deep enough to teach us the lessons as if teaching a primary school student child. Coincidentally she told us that Steve Jobs was a neighbor of hers when in school. Those in her class–like me–became teachers to students of another class; and they were astonished by how easy the subject really was, and yet how difficult it had been portrayed before. Doing, expressing, or using the simple form requires a deep understanding to reach it.

And the last one is pushing for perfection. This is something we may not achieve from the beginning, but we should aim at it in our life. Jobs used it in his products. The reason is because perfection is not something unattainable –it simply means it is complete. The only thing is that sometimes being complete requires digging into its very details. We know when something is finished and perfect when there are not more details to polish. Perfection can be measured by another, but the perfection we talk about is something we know it is perfect: work is over. This is the push we always have to aim at if we are allowed to–and it is worthwhile to achieve it: perfection in our endeavors, perfection in our creations, and perfection in ourselves.

Being the head of others

I want to start with what Moses did that deserved being the leader of a whole nation selected by G-d. We will talk later about different traits and styles, but one simple action was determinant to choose him as the leader: and that was that he cared. Moses was shepherding his sheep while one just got separated and run away. He ran to get it and saw that all it wanted was to drink from a pool of water. Instead of getting angry Moses realized that the sheep was thirsty, so he took compassion and carried it on his shoulders back to the flock. That merited being the shepherd of a nation.

Here we can see that caring about the people we lead is paramount. Only caring we can investigate about their wellbeing, about their progress, about their mishaps, and about the best ways to contribute to the team. Certain leadership roles require getting results, but as we will see later, results without caring only last for so long. Some teams need to be made out of very skilled persons and very matured, yet this does not stop us from the need to care. We are not talking about robots, and yet even with sheep a key feature was to care.

Scriptures pinpoints certain traits that are required for a leader in general. Among them we find wisdom: which means that dominates the issues at hand and the area of leadership as well as the qualities to lead.

Utmost wisdom of the domain one is going to lead is paramount so that all the decisions taken, with its guidance and direction, go to the most optimal path. A leader needs a superior wisdom in the domain that he is going to lead. He has to know more or equal than anybody that he will lead. A good leader needs to be constantly learning to be always at the topmost of the wisdom and knowledge required for his domain.

Joseph became Viceroy of all Egypt with these words from the Pharaoh:

"'Since God has informed you of all this, there can be no one as discerning and wise as you. You shall be in charge of my palace, and by your command shall all my people be sustained; only by the throne shall I outrank to you.' Then Pharaoh said to Joseph, 'See! I have placed you in charge of all the land of Egypt'" (Genesis 41:38-41).

Pharaoh's advisers told him to test Joseph if he knew seventy languages like him. Joseph knew all languages of Pharaoh plus one, Hebrew. That finally settled his position.

Moses was also an example of a holder of the utmost expertise and domain's wisdom. Having acquired the Torah / Bible directly from G-d, he possessed the utmost knowledge of the laws and attitudes that every member of the Israelite nation has to follow wherever they go. His wisdom had to be superior in general to any man that he was going to lead. He was also the conduit for that wisdom —it was meant to be learned by the entire nation.

King David too, as leader and king, was the main transmitter at his time of the sacred wisdom to the following generation. His sacred wisdom was the highest in all Israel. Indeed, king David deduced where the temple had to be built without the exact knowledge of its location, since it was untold on purpose for protection. It was meant to be discovered by him with discerning wisdom.

King Salomon was known for his superior wisdom, knowledge, and understanding. He used his wisdom to lead Israel to be the highest nation in peace and prosperity among all the surrounding nations. He managed to be at that time the ruler of the entire world by marrying daughters of kings of other nations, and by using all his wisdom.

Another quality paramount for a leader found in scriptures is humility. Is humility a sign of weakness? The answer is no.

Humility means that we know our faults and we know our strengths. It means that we are true with the reasons we are where we are and we have what we have–and one of them is that we are meant to use them for our job and for our role. Humility means that we accept rebuke and we improve ourselves. Humility means that we are not affected by others, because we know ourselves; and we know what we do good and not so good without fear, without shame, and with our fullest conviction. Humility is also an awareness that, as we have something, it could also be taken away if decreed. Only with humility we listen to others, we learn, we improve, and we lead with confidence and strength.

Moses was not only the greatest prophet of all time, but the leader of the whole nation of Israel with this quality given in scriptures: "exceedingly humble, more than any person on the face of the earth!" (Numbers 12:3) This quality was not only a necessity to be appointed leader by G-d, but he carried it even while he was tested profoundly by the whole nation. At no moment he showed disdain, pride, conceit, contempt, or self-importance. Indeed, when

G-d wanted to restart again and rebuild Israel with him after the golden calf, Moses pleaded sincerely and eagerly to forgive Israel and preserve the whole nation.

Daniel Goleman has spent a big part of his life researching about Emotional Intelligence [66]. Leadership is one of the areas where his research has brought most attention. In several of his books [67] [68] he shows that in a study of more than three thousand executives from all around the world, six common leadership styles with its different emotional intelligent traits are the determinants of the wellbeing of the team–and of a higher success of up to twenty percent more when used. The most successful ones, moreover, used a different style depending on the situation –even combining them in the same week.

By order of how positive they are they found that authoritative leaders mobilize people towards a vision; coaching leaders develop people for the future; democratic leaders build consensus through participation; affiliative leaders create emotional bonds and harmony; pacesetting leaders expect excellence and self-direction; and coercive leaders demand immediate compliance.

The higher the rank, the more influences the rest. Authoritative leader's style stands out in that a vision is shared among the team [69]. Or the vision of a higher leader is shared, or a specific vision for the team can be used, but having a vision or the ultimate goal to transmit to the team is crucial for focus and efficiency. Moses displayed this authoritative style clearly endowing all the nation with a vision of where they were going, why, and to what they were destined to. When a vision is shared, everybody knows where the destination or the ultimate reason of the work is.

Coaching was also extensively practiced by Moses. He transmitted the wisdom he got to the leaders of the tribes, who themselves transmitted it to the people. He also coached very closely to Joshua, who himself would become later the leader of the nation when Moses died. Coaching is not only needed to transmit information, but also to help any member to catch up with the team and to better develop innate skills aligning the goals of the individual with the group.

Democratic leadership is a trait used overall when a leader wants to take counseling. Any leader, overall of a nation or a wide range of diverse areas, should always take counseling from experts, or just assess if somebody has better ideas. Moses was counseled by Jethro to relegate duties to others by creating a hierarchical way of judging. Using a democratic style is always necessary to get ideas and to assess one's leadership.

Affiliative leadership is used overall to unite a team. Aaron, the high priest, was a key counselor of the nation. Aaron was particularly adept at hearing people's problems and creating peace by understanding their issues, giving counseling, and uniting people. Such traits are essential to maintain the morale and union. They can be used by the leader; or also by a secondary leader that can help if necessary, as Aaron helped Moses. Affiliative style involves taking an assessment of the feelings and creating harmony and union.

Pacesetting leadership is a type of leadership that Goleman argues should be taken only on very specific setups. Once the team is already motivated, united, matured, and very skilled, the leader can higher the productivity by himself setting an example, participating in tasks, and expecting that the rest of the team follow his lead. This leadership style helps outperform, but if not united with other styles it can be distant, expect too much from some members, or not use all their potential nor recognize all their talents and good work. Unless all the team members are motivated and know exactly what to do, it could demoralize a team very easily. King David used this style while in battle, like most militaries may do. He gained close followers using other affiliative styles, yet he also won close strong detractors that wanted to usurp his reign.

Finally, the coercive leadership style, as bad as it sounds, is ideal for emergency moments or for a needed change of course. Only to use in necessary moments or situations, the coercive style just dictates what must be done, fast, direct, and immediate–without questions and with determination. It certainly is necessary at moments, but undermines fast the morale if overused. When Moses transmitted the laws to the nation he had to be direct and understood clearly. Only with determination people could follow. Rehoboam on the other hand, when succeeding King Solomon, did not want to hear advice from the elder council. He put very high taxes on the people as a decree, and with such galling attitude that it resulted in a revolt and the splitting of the country in two.

When leading, there are certain traits that Goleman understands as basic. These are being able to understand our feelings and ourselves emotionally; being able to self-regulate those feelings when needed; empathy with the feelings of other persons–which means understanding what they must be feeling or what feelings would be expected; and finally socializing–which is the ability to hear other persons and to connect, even if there is no immediate plan nor it is related with an immediate labor need that necessitates those interactions.

When leading, understanding others' feelings is important so that everybody work at their best. We are humans after all, and if we are distressed, too stressed, or we do not really see what the value of all we do is, very difficultly we perform at the best of our abilities. If a leader is able to understand this and encourages the team, the workflow is more efficient.

The job of any leader is to understand the task at hand, have all the wisdom and skills necessary to perform it, and direct a team or persons to its consecution–yet he also needs to set an example. It is known from Goleman's research that the leaders at the top affect greatly all the persons of the chain below. The reason is people are more focused on them, and any feeling or disposition is rapidly transmitted–or even emulated.

Being a leader is being human too. Understanding our feelings; being able to reign them; and transmitting the correct feelings to others is key for a whole positive environment. There is no doubt that a combination of traits is needed for different occasions–or are recommended– but the overall positive mindset needs to be cultivated if we expect results.

Any vision that a leader has is transmitted rapidly to the rest. If the leader is positive, the rest is positive; if the leader is courageous, the rest is courageous; if the leader trusts the team, they trust in themselves too–the inherent need to trust that our endeavor will succeed and to trust in the team and ourselves makes trust crucial for resilience, for excellence, and for a huge amount of success.

Without a doubt wisdom is necessary to assess correctly the reality of this positive mindset–what needs to be done and what the domain or the particular leadership position demands in particular–but if the leader does not trust in the particular endeavor, the followers will difficultly join.

Every word uttered to others matters. They can hurt, motivate, or communicate things in one way or another. Respect for people is important. And things that need to be said can be said in a myriad of ways.

A degree of empathy and self-regulation in a leader is important. Being able to quench bad feelings and to communicate correctly is paramount. The need to socialize and to empathize is also necessary because any leader understands that sometimes it is not all about teaching our team or a group of people: but also about communicating; understanding others; and profiting wisdom and resources from our team and other teams, other fields, and other's ideas. Not everything is always fully hierarchical. There is a lot of lateral interaction, even in unexpected ways.

Being head of others implies we are first head of ourselves and we lead others humbly while being wise. The vision clarifies where we are aiming at. The way we behave and interact is looked upon closely; our words encourage or demoralize. Sometimes we must set example; sometimes we must inspire; sometimes we must coach; others hear people replies. Firm commandment is at times in need; and we must always care what other persons feel.

The call to lead: when it is our duty to lead

Ronal Heifetz is his book [70] and his nearly four decades of studying and teaching at the Center for Public Leadership at Harvard Kennedy School, defines leadership as the needed actions to do and to obtain something that is willed, and whose readily available solutions or procedures to get it do not exist yet–requiring hence the creation of changes, learning, and new procedures to be able to obtain it readily, fast, and well from then on.

Any will that we have individually or collectively needs at times to envision, learn, and create new procedures that are not readily available. When the procedures are readily available we are not creating new procedures, but using existing procedures to achieve something–be it because they are already established habits, or because a whole system can do it for us if we demand it or pay for it.

Sometimes to obtain something we may find a mixture of parts that can be acquired by existing procedures, and parts that need the creation of new procedures. It essential to know when we will need new procedures to be able to identify when we will need to exert leadership properly.

When leading there is a resistance to change that happens usually in ourselves and in others, and before we face that resistance we must be equipped with the deep reasons of why it is most pleasurable to pursue a particular will and change. Only then we can discuss it properly, take into account other's opinions, and create necessary changes in the most efficient and beneficial manner with the help of all the stakeholders–those afected represented by their authority figures–involved in the process.

A useful tool to exert leadership is a given authority to demand actions or resources–a defined authority role with its proper contract. Sometimes an authority position does not need to exercise leadership; organizing people to execute known procedures does not involve leadership per se–only when an identified and more desirable will that requires changes and new procedures has been obtained, we can clearly identify the ones that effected that change, and indeed practiced leadership in them and in others.

Another useful tool to exert leadership is the informal authority bestowed by others. Informal authority does not need a contract. It is implied and involves a trust and an expectation of a service in exchange for that trust– the assumed competences and values. At times, though, one can exert leadership without some of these tools–stealthily.

The decision of when to exert leadership is probably one the most shunned and daunting parts when leading others; everybody fears to lose something perceived as invaluable, and it is not always ease to communicate why it is better a change, or how to compromise it best with others.

Skills and values are thus essential: like communicating, sticking to a vision, or mobilizing others with an adamant pursue of the necessary changes to improve something, oneself, or other causes–a sense of duty, and not of honor.

Because "You are not required to complete the task, yet you are not free to withdraw from it." – Pirkey Avot 3, 21. Because "In a place where there are no leaders, strive to be a leader." – Pirkey Avot 2, 6: to grow oneself, to perfect the world, and to guide others–overall our brothers.

16

Give thanks

If he shall offer it for a thanksgiving-offering, he shall offer with the feast thanksgiving-offering unleavened loaves mixed with oil, unleavened wafers smeared with oil, and loaves of scalded fine flour mixed with oil. (Leviticus 7:12)

Being aware of our blessings

When is it proper to say thank you? Gratitude is a feeling that comes when somebody does for us anything that is beyond the expected, beyond the acceptable, and not having done that act would be still considered normal or okay. The person gave beyond the expected out of a pure desire to please us, out of cordiality, or simply from their will to give.

G-d gives us, and in reality does not need anything from us. There are no needs in G-d. All the things we have are purely undeserved. Now, why do we suffer then? The work we do is simply to earn our existence–to earn our being. We may have seen people or kids granted all the riches from their parents. They needed to do nothing. Their life should had been perfect, but at times it was not. That is because on some occasions they did not earn it. Who is rich? The one who enjoys the fruits of his labor–our fights, our growth. These are the fruits: and they will get a reward beyond anything we can imagine in this world. Why do we suffer then? We suffer to correct imperfections and to understand what is right and what is wrong–but this question has puzzled many before.

A week before Israel closed the borders because of COVID-19 I traveled for the first time to Israel. I had no idea this would happen, but I am glad I did it before it escalated to the whole world. I remember I was hesitant at first, but there I was, alone, renting a car, spending three days from Thursday to Monday in a hotel, with no internet, and just the GPS of my phone.

When I visited Jerusalem I remember lots of strange things happening to me: I was mistaken for a Rabi; a couple of persons stopped me asking me for the Temple Institute Museum, and upon discovering how much was of interest I just went myself and it boggled my mind. And just when I decided that I was ready to face the sacred Western Wall, a woman stopped me asking for food and I just bought her and her mother a good kosher meal from a nearby restaurant. She in gratitude asked my name, and upon hearing David occurred to her to show me the way to King David's tomb.

Upon arriving to the tomb I prayed with people there, and it happened to be night. In that beautiful stoned patio we all praised G-d for the crescent moon. Upon my astonishment they invited me to study Torah in a yeshiva that night. I joined a hall full of students–all young and thriving–and they happened to have an exam that night. I did the exam. Afterwards I just left; it was a cold winter and it was late.

Finally, I was ready to face the Western Wall. It was quieter than during the day. Though there are always people praying, I was just privy to more solitude than would be usual, and I enjoyed sitting comfortably on the inner part of the Wall. After praying a little bit there in that encouraging environment it was getting late and I decided to go back to my hotel in Tel-Aviv to check-out and take my flight home. Before leaving I just faced the Wall for the first time, and I inclined my head touching the Wall. The only thing that came to my mind were not supplications for anything I was not having, nor asking for others–which arguably I could have done. The only thing I could say when knowing I was facing His presence and I was at His home was, "Thank you G-d for creating us all." That's it, just "thank you" with all my heart, and I just left the Wall.

I tell this story because that is the only thing we can give to our Creator: a thank you note; an offering; a dedication that acknowledges the myriad of things we have and that we do not necessarily deserve. All we have, all the help, all the blessings are a mere act of love. We usually focus on what we are missing, But are we aware of all that we have in our lives? It is an act of consciousness to be aware of all the good things that we have when we wake up: all the health that we have and that sustain us, be it completely or enough; our meals; our clothes; our homes; our jobs. It is a moral obligation on all of us to be aware of all these blessings; yet the thanksgiving-offerings are always optional. Because thanking cannot be mandated: it can only come from our hearts.

When we search deeply in our hearts and we realize all we have, we can only face down to the floor and give our best thanksgiving-offerings: the offering of our minds, the offering of our actions, the offering of our words, and the offering of our hearts.

Thanking honestly and from our hearts

We all have been taught to say thank you. Just saying, "Thank you very much, I appreciate it", is enough to create a chain reaction in the receiver's heart. We should be used to thank people. We can thank with words, we can thank with actions, we can thank with our hearts, and we can thank with our thoughts.

Are we all aware of all that our parents did for us? How they suffered, how they fought, and how much they compromised? Just giving us life is reason enough to say "Thank you very much." Are we aware how much our spouses, our family, or our friends compromise? We are surrounded by acts of kindness that deserve a thank you from all our hearts. Not everybody acts out of selfishness. There is genuine goodness out there. And our best way to correspond is by acknowledging this and saying, "Thank you very much."

People help each other, there is respect, appreciation, and it is good that we keep the habit of saying "thank you" to those around. A lot of times people help from their hearts–it is their nature. And most of the time nothing else is expected from us; nor returning the favor; nor keeping track of the good act. Sometimes the only thing expected is a heartfelt real "Thank you very much."

I was once saved from a swimming pool drowned–from deep in the water with my heart just stopped. The guy who took me out was fired. I never had the chance to tell him, "Thank you very much." The doctor who saved my life just got nonsense from me, and I could not utter anything worth a dime. Yet, I never got the chance to meet her again, and the only thing I could think of is my deepest, "Thank you very much." The teacher who told me those harsh words woke me up from my slumber–she woke me up in my mind. I never really dared to say to her the reality, "Thank you really very much."

I met people in university that changed my life; other persons veered my course to the right path. Undoubtedly they all deserve a big "Thank you very much." Some friends became an anchor, and unbeknown to them I grew while they made me laugh. Certainly I should go and tell them, "Thank you really very much." Some persons not now with us contributed on my education choice and were essential for my growth, wisdom, and insight; and I must say that they deserve always a big "Thank you very much."

I was once accepted in a community that helped me grow and used all their wisdom and heart. It is obvious to them that they also deserve a big "Thank you very much."

I worked with excellent people that only showed comprehension, and I always appreciated their wisdom and their smile. It is clear that I must also say to them, "Thank you very much."

My family has always been there—when things were good and when things were bad. They will always have from my heart a real "Thank you very much." A friend helped me writing this book; and many more help me with only needing to ask. To them I truly say "Thank you very much."

For all of you who dared to read my book, certainly you are one of a kind; only those who learn from others can be really labelled as wise. A few things may be useful to some, others may use the whole bunch, but there is no doubt in anybody that we all want to grow up and thrive. I just hope with all my heart that all goes well and all our dreams come alive. May G-d be lauded eternally, and we all acknowledge His might. One thing is sure, I am indebted to you all for reading all my advice, and there is no best way to tell it to you than saying to you deeply and honestly a heartfelt, "Thank you very much."

iStockphoto.com/ricocheet64

NOTES

[1] *Zohar, parashat Vayeira*

[2] Christopher Francese. (2007). *Ancient Rome in So Many Words.* Hippocrene Books, pp. 76

[3] Witold Rybczynski. (August 1991). *Waiting for the Weekend.* The Atlantic. pp. 35-52.

[4] A Schroeder, G. (2011). *Genesis and the Big Bang Theory: The Discovery Of Harmony Between Modern Science And The Bible.* Random House Publishing Group

[5] Ashby N. (2003). *Relativity in the Global Positioning System.* Living Rev Relativ.

[6] Laura Pilossoph and Shu Lin Wee. (2021). *Household Search and the Marital Wage Premium.* American Economic Journal: Macroeconomics

[7] *Seder Olam Rabbah 2*

[8] *Ketubot* 105b

[9] Mel Robbins. (2017). T*he 5 Second Rule: Transform your Life, Work, and Confidence with Everyday Courage.* Savio Republic

[10] Ramhal. (1738). *Mesillat Yesharim: The path of the just.*

[11] *Proverbs* 12:26

[12] *Judges* 13-16

[13] *Avodah Zarah* 19a:14

[14] *Proverbs* 22:4

[15] *Sanhedrin* 106a

[16] *Pirkei DeRabbi Eliezer*

[17] *Megillah* 12a:9-15

[18] *Avodah Zarah* 54a:4

[19] Zvi Ron. (2021). *The Nuremberg Trial in Megillat Esther.* DOI:10.1093/mj/kjaa019

[20] Sian E. Harding. (2024). *The Exquisite Machine: The New Science of the Heart.* The MIT Press

[21] J. L. Ardell and J. A. Armour. (2016). *Neurocardiology: Structure-Based Function.* Comprehensive Physiology 6 : 1635-1653.

[22] Juanjuan Zhao, Liming Pei. (2020). *Cardiac Endocrinology: Heart-Derived Hormones in Physiology and Disease.* Transl Sci. 5(9):949-960.

[23] McCraty R. (2015). *Science of the heart: exploring the role of the heart in human performance.* Boulder Creek: HeartMath Institute

[24] Alshami AM. (2019). *Pain: Is It All in the Brain or the Heart?.* Current Pain and Headache Reports. 23(12):88.

[25] James Nestor. (2020). *Breath: The New Science of a Lost Art.* Riverhead Books.

[26] Priyaranjan Biswal, Prases K. Mohanty. (2021). *Development of quadruped walking robots: A review.* Ain Shams Engineering Journal, Vol 12, Issue 2, pp. 2017-2031.

[27] Charles Duhigg. (2012). *The Power of Habit: Why we do what we do and how to change.* Random House

[28] James Clear. (2018). *Atomic habits: An Easy & Proven Way to Build Good Habits & Break Bad Ones.* Avery.

29 Stephen Guise. (2021). *Elastic Habits: How to Create Smarter Habits That Adapt to Your Day.* Selective Entertainment LLC

30 Spindler LRB, Luppi AI, Adapa RM, *et al.* (2021). *Dopaminergic brainstem disconnection is common to pharmacological and pathological consciousness perturbation.* Proc Natl Acad Sci USA. 118(30).

31 Daniel Z. Lieberman and Michael E. Long. (2018) *The Molecule of More: How a Single Chemical in Your Brain Drives Love, Sex, and Creativity—and Will Determine the Fate of the Human Race.* BenBella Books, Inc.

32 Jeffrey M. Schwartz , Rebecca Gladding. (2011) *You Are Not Your Brain: The 4-Step Solution for Changing Bad Habits, Ending Unhealthy Thinking, and Taking Control of Your Life.* Avery.

33 Banks, E., Joshy, G., Weber, M.F. *et al.* (2015). *Tobacco smoking and all-cause mortality in a large Australian cohort study: findings from a mature epidemic with current low smoking prevalence.* BMC Med 13, 38.

34 Dongelmans, M., Durand-de Cuttoli, R., Nguyen, C. *et al.* (2021). *Chronic nicotine increases midbrain dopamine neuron activity and biases individual strategies towards reduced exploration in mice.* Nat Commun 12, 6945.

35 Allen Carr, John Dicey. (2020). *Allen Carr's Easy Way To Quit Smoking Without Willpower.* Arcturus Publishing Ltd

36 Reynolds, J.N.J., Avvisati, R., Dodson, P.D. *et al.* (2022). *Coincidence of cholinergic pauses, dopaminergic activation and depolarisation of spiny projection neurons drives synaptic plasticity in the striatum.* Nat Commun 13, 1296

[37] Walker, M. (2018). *Why we sleep: The new science of sleep and dreams*. Penguin Books

[38] Calvo Tapia, C., Tyukin, I. & Makarov, V.A. (2020). *Universal principles justify the existence of concept cells*. Sci Rep 10, 7889.

[39] Stanford University Medical Center. (November 2010). *Stunning details of brain connections revealed*. ScienceDaily

[40] Lauren Aguirre. (2021). *The Memory Thief: And the Secrets Behind How We Remember–A Medical Mystery*. Pegasus Books

[41] Cheval, B., Darrous, L., Choi, K.W. *et al.* (2023). *Genetic insights into the causal relationship between physical activity and cognitive functioning. Sci Rep* 13, 5310

[42] Casey Means, MD. (2024). *Good Energy: The Surprising Connection Between Metabolism and Limitless Health*. Avery.

[43] *Numbers* 6

[44] *Devarim* 21

[45] Anna Lembke. (2021). *Dopamine Nation: Finding Balance in the Age of Indulgence*. Dutton

[46] Micha R, Wallace SK, Mozaffarian D. (2010). *Red and processed meat consumption and risk of incident coronary heart disease, stroke, and diabetes mellitus: a systematic review and meta-analysis*. Circulation.;121(21):2271-83.

[47] Willett WC, Ludwig DS. (2020). *Milk and Health*. N Engl J Med. 382(7):644-654.

48 Soltani, Jayedi, Shab-Bidar, Becerra-Tomás, Salas-Salvadó. (2019). *Adherence to the Mediterranean Diet in Relation to All-Cause Mortality: A Systematic Review and Dose-Response Meta-Analysis of Prospective Cohort Studies.* Adv Nutr. 10(6):1029-1039.

49 Pattnaik H, Mir M, Boike S, Kashyap R, Khan SA, Surani S. (2022). *Nutritional Elements in Sleep.* Cureus. 14(12).

50 Marie Kondo. (2014). *The life-changing magic of tidying up.* Ten Speed Press

51 Stephen Guise. (2013). *Mini Habits: Smaller Habits, Bigger Results.* CreateSpace Independent Publishing Platform

52 Stephen R. Covey. (2013). *The 7 Habits of Highly Effective People - Powerful Lessons in Personal Change.* Free Press

53 Jim Kwik. (2020). *Limitless: Upgrade Your Brain, Learn Anything Faster, and Unlock Your Exceptional Life.* Hay House, Inc

54 Robert Kegan, Lisa Laskow Lahey. (2009). *Immunity to Change: How to Overcome it and Unlock Potential in Yourself and Your Organization.* Harvard Business Press.

55 *Avot D'Rabbi Natan* 34:9

56 Meik Wiking. (2016). *Little Book Of Hygge: The Danish Way to Live Well.* DK

57 Ghosh, S. K. (2018). *Happy Hormones at Work: Applying the Learnings from Neuroscience to Improve and Sustain Workplace Happiness.* NHRD Network Journal. 11. 83-92.

58 Napoleon Hill. (1937). *Think and Grow Rich.* The Ralston Society

59 Viktor E. Frankel. (1946). *Man's Search for Meaning.* Beacon Press

60 Bonini L, Rotunno C, Arcuri E, Gallese V. (2022). *Mirror neurons 30 years later: implications and applications.* Trends Cogn Sci. Vol 26, Issue 9, pp. 767-781.

61 *Genesis* 31:32

62 *Tallelei Orot, Shemot,* 2:14, p.52.

63 Reber P. (May 2010). *What Is the Memory Capacity of the Human Brain?.* "Ask the Brains" in Scientific American. Mind Vol. 21 No. 2 p. 70.

64 Walter Isaacson. (April 2012). *The Real Leadership Lessons of Steve Jobs.* Harvard Business Review

65 Gary Keller, Jay Papasan. (2013). *The ONE Thing: The Surprisingly Simple Truth About Extraordinary Results.* Bard

66 Daniel Goleman. (1995). *Emotional Intelligence: Why It Can Matter More Than IQ.* Bantam

67 Daniel Goleman. (2011). *Leadership: The Power of Emotional Intelligence.* More Than Sound

68 Daniel Goleman. (2014). *What Makes a Leader: Why Emotional Intelligence Matters.* More Than Sound

69 Simon Sinek. (2011). *Start with Why: How Great Leaders Inspire Everyone to Take Action.* Portfolio

70 Ronald A. Heifetz, Marty Linsky, Alexander Grashow. (2009) *The Practice of Adaptive Leadership: Tools and Tactics for Changing Your Organization and the World.* Harvard Business Press